'The book every wage slave needs to turn their early retirement dreams into a reality.'

Mike Southon, co-author of 'The Beermat Entrepreneur' and other business books

'Financial planning puts clients' needs first and helps them to achieve their financial and lifestyle goals. Retirement is not about preparing to die but taking advantage of another stage in life. Proper preparation will ensure that these goals are met. This book approaches planning for retirement in a refreshingly modern and candid way.'

Nick Cann, Chief Executive, Institute of Financial Planning

'Sound financial advice in a crazy world is often in scant supply. This book delivers it in spades. If he had written it 10 years ago, I would now be happily retired!'

Jeff Prestridge, Personal Finance Editor, Financial Mail on Sunday

'Early retirement doesn't happen by accident, it happens by exercising control and planning. If you really want to, you can make it happen; this book will help you achieve that goal.'

Tom McPhail, Head of Pensions Research, Hargreaves Lansdown

'Once again, Martin has delivered a no-nonsense, jargon-free guide to managing your finances. Retiring early is a dream for many, but this practical book shows how, by taking several straightforward steps, it can be ~~~~~~~~~~~~'

Melanie Wright, awar~ 700031658524

'When most people are worryi~~~~~~~~~~~~~~~~~~ be able to retire, it is refreshing to read a positive and practical book that can help you escape the rat race 10 years early. The early retirement check list is a fantastic guide to the things you should start doing right now to get on an even financial keel, regardless of whether you want to stop work ~r n~t.'

Jill Insley, Cash and Propert

D0273368

How to Retire 10 Years Early

Prentice Hall LIFE

If life is what you make it, then making it better starts here.

What we learn today can change our lives tomorrow. It can change our goals or change our minds; open up new opportunities or simply inspire us to make a difference. That's why we have created a new breed of books that do more to help you make more of *your* life.

Whether you want more confidence or less stress, a new skill or a different perspective, we've designed *Prentice Hall Life* books to help you to make a change for the better. Together with our authors we share a commitment to bring you the brightest ideas and best ways to manage your life, work and wealth.

In these pages we hope you'll find the ideas you need for the life *you* want. Go on, help yourself.

It's what you make it

* * *

How to Retire 10 Years Early

Your Plan for Less Work and More Life

Martin Bamford

PEARSON
Prentice Hall
LIFE

Harlow, England • London • New York • Boston • San Francisco • Toronto • Sydney • Singapore • Hong Kong
Tokyo • Seoul • Taipei • New Delhi • Cape Town • Madrid • Mexico City • Amsterdam • Munich • Paris • Milan

PEARSON EDUCATION LIMITED

Edinburgh Gate
Harlow CM20 2JE
Tel: +44 (0)1279 623623
Fax: +44 (0)1279 431059
Website: www.pearsoned.co.uk

First published in Great Britain in 2008

© Informed Choice Ltd 2008

The right of Martin Bamford to be identified as author of this work has been asserted
by him in accordance with the Copyright, Designs and Patents Act 1988.

ISBN: 978–0–273–71427–9

British Library Cataloguing-in-Publication Data
A catalogue record for this book is available from the British Library.

Library of Congress Cataloging-in-Publication Data
Bamford, Martin.
  How to retire 10 years early : your plan for less work and more life / Martin Bamford.
    p. cm.
  Includes index.
  ISBN 978-0-273-71427-9 (alk. paper)
  1. Finance, Personal. 2. Retirement income--Planning. 3. Investments. I. Title. II. Title:
How to retire ten years early.
  HG179.B287 2008
  332.024'014--dc22
                          2007039399

10 9 8 7 6 5 4 3 2 1
11 10 09 08 07

Typeset in 10pt IowanOldStyl
Printed in Great Britain by He

The Publisher's policy is to us

Contents

CHAPTER 01

CHAPTER 02

The alternatives to early retirement 168

Your early retirement checklist 180

About the author

Martin has been an independent financial adviser for five years and is joint managing director of professional advisory firm Informed Choice Ltd. At only 28 years old, he already holds the Advanced Financial Planning Certificate from the Chartered Insurance Institute (CII). He is an Associate of the Personal Finance Society and also of the Institute of Financial Planning.

His first book, *The Money Tree*, was published in 2006 by Pearson Prentice Hall and became the WHSmith Business Book of the Month.

He is no stranger to the media, writing for *FS Focus*, *Canary Wharf City Life*, *Money Marketing* and *IFAonline*. He is regularly quoted in the national press, including the *Telegraph*, *The Observer*, *The Times* and *The Independent*. In his capacity as a financial expert, Martin has been a regular guest on BBC and commercial radio.

In September 2006, Martin was named as one of the most influential independent financial advisers in Britain by *Professional Adviser* magazine. His firm, Informed Choice, is one of only two firms offering independent financial advice in the UK to have received the Gold Standard for Independent Financial Advice at the Gold Standard Awards 2006. In January 2007, Martin was a finalist for IFA Personality of the Year at the Professional Adviser Awards.

Martin lives in Surrey with his wife and their baby daughter. In his spare time, Martin enjoys walking in the countryside, scuba-diving and fly fishing.

Thank you

My daughter is the reason for writing this book and my wife has made this book possible. Thank you to Megan and Lindie.

I would also like to thank my colleagues at Informed Choice who make early retirement a possibility for our clients on a daily basis.

Thank you to all the readers of my first book, *The Money Tree*, and particularly those who have been in touch to ask me to keep writing.

Last, but not least, thank you to Sam Jackson and her team at Pearson Prentice Hall for continuing to work their magic on my words.

Thank you all.

Introduction

> Age is something that doesn't matter, unless you are a cheese.
>
> Billie Burke (1885–1970)

Welcome to the book that can cut 10 years off your working life and make early retirement a reality.

The old notion of retirement is dead.

The old notion of retirement is dead. It is no longer a day in the distant future when, on reaching your sixty-fifth birthday, you hang up your suit and never return to the office again. Retirement has become a complicated and challenging gradual phasing out of work and phasing in of leisure time.

Through my work as a financial planner I have been able to develop a real insight into retirement, what it means and how to make it happen sooner.

This book is here to show you that it is both possible and desirable to be in the financial position to retire 10 years early. It will show you how to make this happen.

Being in this enviable financial position 10 years early will give you more choice. It will give you choices about when and where you work as you get older. The Retire 10 Years Early (RTYE) plan will give you control over both of these factors in your old age.

Why this book?

I had to think long and hard before writing this book. We are all bombarded with ways to pay off our debts in three years or become a property millionaire in eight years. This book had to strike the right balance between being ambitious and being realistic.

> **Most people I speak to are oblivious when it comes to their retirement planning.**

The RTYE plan is still ambitious – there is no disputing that – but most people I speak to are oblivious when it comes to their retirement planning. Minimal thought appears to have gone into it. They don't have an accurate handle on what they can expect when they retire or even when that might be.

We are all being told that we need to work for longer and retire later. The Government seems constantly to be dealing with a 'pensions crisis' and its solutions involve making our retirement take place later than ever before.

Fortunately, the Government doesn't decide how many years you have to work for or when you can retire. Personal choice still exists in our society and a growing number of people choose to take advantage of the fact. They come to me with ambitious plans to retire at 55 or even 45 years old. They know that, with a well thought through and executed plan in place, almost anything is possible.

I won't claim that it is easy to retire 10 years early. It's not easy to repay your mortgage in a short space of time either, but people make it happen. It's not easy to quit your safe job and start your own business, but people make it happen. If early retirement is something you are determined that you really want, you will find a way to make it happen.

Now for the good news – the RTYE plan is incredibly simple. Making sure that you have all of the skills and tools in place to make this simple plan a reality is the challenging part, but I'm on hand to guide you through any difficulties associated with early retirement planning. Together we can make it more than a distinct possibility – we can make it a reality.

I have tried to write this book in a way that retains the simplicity of the RTYE plan but, at the same time, reflects the hard work it takes to achieve such a big challenge. Within each chapter, I have started with the basics and then moved on to more complicated areas. By the end of each chapter, you will be learning more advanced techniques to enable you to implement the RTYE plan.

Why bother?

It's easy to dismiss retirement planning. Many people do. The huge number of financial pressures we all face today often force retirement planning to the bottom of our collective financial agenda. I'm sure that we all have more important things to spend the money on.

We have to:

- repay debt accumulated while studying in higher education
- clear credit cards from those early years of employment when the monthly salary never seemed to be enough to maintain our lavish lifestyles
- save for a deposit on a house as property prices continue to run away from us
- finance the cost of starting and raising a family
- repay our substantial mortgages and stay on top of the monthly budget when the interest rates rise.

This list completely neglects all of the other items constantly vying for our financial attention – the foreign holidays, new cars, eating out, clothes and consumer electronics.

> **If you follow this plan, you will be in control of your own financial destiny.**

Our cash is always in demand and this fact will never change, unless you make it change. If you dismiss retirement planning, you will reach retirement with only the State to bail you out. If you follow this plan, you will be back in control of your own financial destiny. That's not a difficult choice to make.

It's not just about the cash

Retirement is not just about money. While the financial aspect of retirement plays an important part, other factors are just as important. Making the transition from work to life can wake you up with a jolt. This transition can even put a strain on previously happy relationships.

> **Retirement is not just about money.**

In Japan, 'retired husband syndrome' has led to a massive rise in the divorce rate. Japanese men are starting to discover that, after a lifetime of long hours away at the office, they don't like spending too much time with their wives. Equally, combined with an increase in life expectancy, Japanese women are deciding in their droves that a lengthy retirement spent in close proximity to their previously absent husbands is too much to handle.

Other nations are quickly facing up to this problem. In the UK, we are witnessing the rise of 'retirement coaches' who help the newly retired plan the more holistic aspects of their life in retirement. I have recently worked with clients who were sent away on a two-day residential course to better understand how to deal with the transition from employee to full-time house husband.

Ann Harrison is a certified retirement options coach at ContemporaryRetirementCoaching.com. Ann says:

If you're planning an early retirement, it is vital that you give equal consideration to planning the non-financial aspects of retirement. How successful you are at recreating the feelings of satisfaction, importance, usefulness, companionship and productivity that you previously obtained from your work will be crucial to your well-being and happiness in the next phase of your life.

Failure to consider the physical, mental, emotional and spiritual implications of early retirement has sent many early retirees in the direction of the JobCentre (or their doctor's surgery).

Reasons to retire early

Your motivation for an early retirement is likely to be very personal. Our reasons vary as much as our tastes in music, favourite holiday destinations or choice of car.

When conducting some research for this book, I asked some friends what they would do if they could retire 10 years early. Here are some of their answers to give you a flavour of the range of different ideas people have for an early retirement.

- Select a new subject to study and stretch the mind a little more.
- Write more and watch the sun set more often. But, really, I think I would carry on doing what I do now except I wouldn't have to charge or get so booked up!

- Get my pottery studio going again.

- I don't really have a clear notion of when I am likely to retire so it's hard to say, but I would like to spend some time doing something more enriching than my present career while I still have some energy.

- Have thought of teaching one day.

- Go and live in France, of course!

- All the things I feel I don't have time to do! Travel round Italy (by train – carbon footprint friendly!), set up my own ceramics studio so I could sculpt to my heart's content, maybe do a zoology/ecology degree.

As you can see from these comments, ideas for the contents of an early retirement vary quite a lot.

What would you do if you could retire 10 years early? The possibilities are endless.

> What would you do if you could retire 10 years early?

What you will find in this book

The structure of this book is designed to be easy and practical to follow. Here's a brief roller-coaster ride of what you will find.

After this Introduction, we start off in Chapter 1 looking at what early retirement means. Retirement means different things to different people. Early retirement also has a variable definition depending on your perspective.

Retirement has changed a great deal over the past 50 years. In Chapter 1 we look at the reasons for these changes and why this matters to your early retirement plans.

Chapter 2 is all about preparation, to get you ready for the RTYE plan. I will explain what you need to know and do to make this plan a reality. We also spend some time looking at the mindset you need if you are to implement the RTYE plan. It's an important chapter because, without putting down a proper foundation, there is a real danger that your plan will fail.

The contents of Chapter 3 start to introduce the practical parts of the RTYE plan. Budgeting is the crucial first step and will very quickly give you a good idea of what you can achieve. It should be simple to budget, but people still make common mistakes that can reduce the effectiveness of the exercise. We look at these common mistakes and the assumptions that you will need to make as you build your own RTYE plan.

One of the most effective ways to make the RTYE plan come to life is to destroy your debt. Clearing your mortgage is one of the most effective uses of your financial resources as you work through the RTYE plan. In Chapter 4 I share some of the strategies you can use to speed up the repayment of your mortgage and why this makes such a big difference.

Chapter 5 is all about the financial vehicles you will need to understand and use for a smooth ride to an early retirement. I describe the range of financial tools and vehicles you can use to do this.

Pensions (the dreaded 'p' word) are covered but I take a very candid look at their effectiveness in the twenty-first century. I also take a closer look at the non-pension alternatives you need to know about.

Chapter 6 is all about risk. Investment risk can be both the best friend and worst enemy of the RTYE plan. In order to make risk work in your favour, you have to know when is the right time to take more risk and when to move to a more cautious position with your money. In this chapter, I explain how to control risk and stop it from controlling your plans.

In Chapter 7, we look at cutting costs as a method of bringing your retirement date closer. Charges and other costs can destroy your early retirement goals. By shopping around you can usually reduce costs, but how can you tell if you are reducing value as well? Low cost does not always mean good value so, in this chapter, we look at striking the right balance between the two.

Chapter 8 is about getting a helping hand from the taxman. Understanding how tax works and how it can actually contribute to the RTYE plan is an important part of making the plan a reality.

In Chapter 9, we look at ways to keep the RTYE plan on track. It is important to set benchmarks to measure your progress. We look at the best benchmarks to use and how to make them work to your advantage. In this chapter we also explain how to conduct a thorough annual review of your early retirement plans.

Chapter 10 considers the alternatives to an early retirement. The word 'retirement' has grown to have a very personal meaning for different people. In this chapter, we look at how the RTYE plan can be beneficial for you if you *don't* want to retire 10 years early – or even 10 years late!

Finally, we finish the book with your early retirement checklist – the 50 points that you have to cover to make your early retirement plan a roaring success. Think of this as a 'super-summary' of the book, designed to get you revved up for action.

A word of warning

Before you read on, I must give you a brief word of warning about the way I do things. I like to get straight to the point and keep things simple. I like telling people things how they are. You won't find any sugar-coated messages in this book. If there is a bitter pill to deliver, then I will offer it to you with a glass of water and a smile.

> **If there is a bitter pill to deliver, then I will offer it to you with a glass of water and a smile.**

My apologies in advance if you find anything in this book uncomfortable or challenging. It is never my intention to offend people, but my approach sometimes results in this happening. If you are offended, then I'm sure it will pass and you will quickly realise that I'm just being straight with you.

I'm not like any financial adviser you have ever met before. I'm not a stuffy old man in a suit. In fact, I can count on one hand the number of times I've worn a suit in the past five years.

I'm not a poorly qualified salesman looking for the next opportunity to sell a product and earn my commission. I stopped working on that basis almost as soon as I became a financial adviser because it didn't suit my view of the world. My core business now is selling professional advice and planning services to private clients. This sometimes leads to the sale of a financial product but, more often than not, it means the delivery of advice and that's it.

I hope that you enjoying reading this book. More importantly, I hope you find practical value in the knowledge within these pages. Take this book and turn it into your own plan to retire 10 years early. Use this book to turn early retirement from a dream into a reality.

What is early retirement?

> Retirement may be looked upon either as a
> prolonged holiday or as a rejection, a being
> thrown on to the scrap-heap.
>
> Simone de Beauvoir (1908–1986)

01

Understanding 'retirement' used to be easy. It was the day you stopped work completely at 60 years old for women or 65 years old for men. It was a predetermined point in your career when you would stop picking up a salary and start collecting a pension. How things have changed.

> **Understanding 'retirement' used to be easy. How things have changed.**

Retirement today means different things to different people. The State pension age of 65 years old is still in place as a benchmark but, other than that, all bets are off.

More modern pension arrangements give people the ability to mix their benefits with reduced earnings from part-time employment.

Working into your 70s or even 80s is no longer considered unusual. Some employers actively encourage older workers. Pay a visit to your local DIY store one afternoon and check out the age profile of staff. The same is true across many different sectors.

In this chapter, we shall look at what retirement really means and how it has changed.

Changes to the concept of retirement have been largely driven by improved life expectancy. Later in this chapter we talk about how much longer we are all starting to live for and what this means for retirement planning.

Finally, we look at early retirement and what the ability to retire 10 years early really means.

What is retirement?

Retirement is the period of a person's life during which they are no longer working. The word is more commonly used to describe the start of that period of life – the one day when you move from working to being retired.

Our own perceptions of what it means to retire and be retired differ, but there are some common themes. If you say 'retirement' to people, you might expect them to think about queuing in the Post Office to pick up their State pension, bus passes and mobility assistance.

Whatever we might think about retirement, it is a clear phase in our lives. It should be a time when our priorities change from earning money to spending more time with family and generally relaxing. For this reason, it is a very important time in our lives. For most people it is a well-deserved break from a long and demanding career.

These traditional perceptions of retirement have been changing as a result of better life expectancy, better health during retirement and access to a wider range of options later in life. People now regard retirement as a new and very active phase of their lives. This might involve personal development, a change to a new career or even a complete reinvention of your life. As a result, it is potentially a very exciting time.

> People now regard retirement as a new and very active phase of their lives.

What is early retirement?

Because we don't have a clear idea of what 'retirement' means, it is difficult to define what 'early retirement' means. The term used to mean stopping work earlier than the traditional retirement ages of 60 for women or 65 for men. Someone who stopped work and picked up a pension at 58 years old would be classed as an early retiree under this old definition.

The new definition is far vaguer. If there is not a clear definition of retirement, just about anything could be considered a normal retirement age or, indeed, an early retirement age.

The purpose of this book is to put you in the position to retire 10 years earlier than you would have been able to if you had taken no action. This means that your personal definition of a normal retirement age will dictate what early retirement means to you.

For many people, it will mean 10 years earlier than the normal retirement age for their company pension scheme. The age of 65 is a commonly accepted pension scheme retirement age for both men and women these days. Retiring at 55 years old would certainly be considered 'early'.

Maybe you already had a more ambitious target than normal of retiring at 60 or 55 years old. Retiring 10 years early for you will therefore mean an even more ambitious goal of a retirement age of 50 or even 45 years old.

A lot will depend on your age now, your existing plans for retirement and your general attitudes towards retirement and early retirement. If you had little in the way of existing plans or provision for retirement, then early retirement might mean hanging up your briefcase at 60 years old.

There is no single retirement age that everyone will agree on as being typical. Pick your own original retirement age and then

> There are no right or wrong answers when it comes to deciding on the best age to retire.

base the RTYE plan on that. There are no right or wrong answers when it comes to deciding on the best age to retire. Having clear plans is far more important.

Myths about retirement

Before we talk about early retirement, it is important to know about some of the commonest retirement myths. These are all things I have been told in the past by friends and clients. You need to be aware of them so you do not fall into the trap of thinking they are things that will happen to you. Here are my six top myths about retirement.

Retirement myth 1: The State will look after me

The State pension exists to keep people from living in total poverty when they retire. If all you have to live on during retirement is a State pension, you will have a fairly meagre existence to look forward to.

> If all you have to live on during retirement is a State pension, you will have a fairly meagre existence.

A life assurance company recently conducted an experiment, asking adults to try and live on the equivalent of the State pension for one week. The experiment started on a Thursday (when the State pension is paid each week) and all of the households that took part had run out of money by lunchtime on Sunday.

The basic State pension is just under £90 a week. To this you can add any additional State pension (known as the State Second Pension), which is based on the National Insurance contributions you have made during your working life. There is also a means-tested (income-related) payment that should ensure anyone over 65 years old receives around £120 a week (if single) or £180 a week (if he or she has a partner).

Retirement myth 2: There is no tax to pay during retirement

This myth ranks right up there with the one about children and students not having to pay income tax when they earn money. We *all* have to pay income tax when we earn money, regardless of our age.

It's true that certain tax breaks improve as we get older, but retired people pay tax just like everybody else. They pay income tax on their income from pensions, employment, savings and investments. They pay capital gains tax when they sell certain assets for more than they bought them for. Their beneficiaries pay inheritance tax when they die.

Retired people pay tax just like everybody else.

More of your income is free of tax as you get older. This is the tax break known as a personal allowance. We all have a personal allowance, which means that the first part of our income each year is free of tax. It goes up by about 45 per cent on your sixty-fifth birthday and then by a small amount on your seventy-fifth birthday. However, this increased personal allowance is connected to an income limit that can reduce the personal allowance back down to the original level.

Retirement myth 3: My cost of living will be lower when I retire

We shall look at this in more detail in Chapter 3, but, for the most part, it is nonsense. The general expectation that the cost of living during retirement will be lower is not always true.

Certain items of expenditure, such as mortgage payments, no longer apply. However, many of these items of expenditure are quickly replaced by additional costs, such as heating, leisure and travel. Add to this the fact that the cost of living for retired people generally rises faster than the cost of living for people still in work. Retirement is not the cheap option that many people think it will be.

> The cost of living for retired people generally rises faster than the cost of living for people still in work.

Retirement myth 4: My home is my pension

There is a big difference of opinion on this subject. Many people have been dismissing traditional pension plans in recent years because they have seen the value of their main residence grow and grow. Some of the latest research I have seen suggests that as many as 30 per cent of people plan to use their home to supplement their income in retirement.

In order to use the value in your house to supplement your income in retirement, a number of things have to fall into place.

> **Because you will still need a place to live during retirement, the total sale of your property is probably not an option.**

You will need to either sell your house and move to a smaller (cheaper) property or find another way of releasing some of the equity from your property. Because you will still need a place to live during retirement, the total sale of your property is probably not an option. Doing so would release some money but leave you with a significant new item of expenditure – rent – that you would need to pay for the rest of your life.

The biggest danger with this strategy is the expectation that house prices will continue to rise in the future in the same way that they have done in the past. There is a chance that this will happen, but making a big assumption like this and relying on a single asset to fund your retirement is a very high-risk strategy. Your home may well be another asset that can supplement your retirement income, but your home in isolation is not your pension.

Retirement myth 5: You need a massive pension fund to retire in comfort

It's wrong to assume that you need a huge pension fund to retire in comfort unless you have worked this out for yourself. Don't rely on generic guidelines that tell you how much you need to save for retirement. Personalise the calculations based on your own financial position and lifestyle requirements. Until

> **Don't rely on generic guidelines that tell you how much you need to save for retirement.**

you have undertaken a detailed budgeting exercise (more on this in Chapter 3), it is wrong to make assumptions about the size of the pension fund you might need in the future.

Your pension fund requirements will be directly linked to your likely expenditure during retirement and what other sources of capital and income you will have at your disposal. Some advisers like to encourage their clients to work towards a massive pension fund on the basis that it is better to have too much than too little when you come to retire. However, setting impossible targets is a sure-fire way of putting people off any form of saving for retirement. Having realistic and attainable retirement planning targets increases the chances that you will actually keep working towards those goals.

Retirement myth 6: You don't need to plan for retirement because you will continue to work

Just because retirement is no longer a single date when you stop working, it is wrong to assume that you can keep working forever. As we get older, our ability to work diminishes. Yes, there are some 70-year-olds who can work as hard, with the same levels of energy and enthusiasm, as 30-year-olds, but relying on your ability to work until your dying day is not a sensible retirement planning strategy.

Some of the surveys I have seen recently suggest that as many as 80 per cent of people expect to continue working, in one way or another, after they retire. This plan rests on both being able to keep working and the availability of paid work at that time.

It is wrong to assume that you can keep working forever.

There are too many ifs and buts to make this a strategy to completely rely on for your income during retirement.

Just like a house, working in retirement may well be a way of supplementing your other income, but you should not plan to exist solely on the money you can earn in your 60s, 70s, 80s and beyond!

Good news and bad news

Life expectancy is a massive consideration when it comes to retirement planning and particularly early retirement. When it comes to life expectancy and retirement planning, the good news is that we are all living longer. The bad news is that we are all living longer. If you are going to succeed with the RTYE plan, you need to understand the financial risks associated with living longer.

> The good news is that we are all living longer.
> The bad news is that we are all living longer.

Increased life expectancy has both a positive and negative impact on retirement planning. Very few people will complain about the prospect of living longer. More time to spend in retirement sounds like fair compensation for a life of hard work.

The downside of this increased longevity is the cost. Living longer is more expensive. It means that you have to build up a bigger pension fund to provide a reasonable level of income that will last a lifetime. It means that you have to be more prudent with your capital to ensure you can still leave a decent inheritance to your kids. It increases the chances that you will need to pay for long-term care in your old age.

Our parents' generation didn't have these problems. Life expectancy back then was more manageable from a financial perspective. They could work for 40 years and then retire on a reasonable pension designed to last 10 or 15 years.

Life expectancy continues to increase in the developed world as a result of higher living standards and better healthcare. Advancements in medical science also have a role to play.

This ability to live 10, 20 or 30 years longer than our ancestors has a big impact on retirement planning. Living longer is expensive and requires more cash to see you through your retirement.

Rather than splashing out on a brand new car in retirement, with the intention of it being their final car, today's retirees are likely to get through three or four new cars during their retirement. The retirees of tomorrow should consider striking up good relationships with their local car dealers.

It also changes the balance between your working life and your life in retirement.

A word of warning – following the RTYE plan will increase the 'problem' of improved life expectancy. By bringing your retirement date forward 10 years, you will be making the '4-decade retirement' a distinct probability. Living longer is good news and bad news for retirement planning.

We live for longer as we get older

Most of us are familiar with the term 'life expectancy'. It means the number of years the average person can expect to live for when they are born. It is important to remember that it is only an average. This means that half of the people born in a particular year will live for longer than the average life expectancy. Half will die sooner. As individuals we are not average.

As well as life expectancy, it is important to understand the term 'longevity'. It is a bit like life expectancy, but it refers to the length of time an average person can expect to live once he or she has reached a particular age. For example, if a woman celebrated her 70th birthday in 2005, she could expect – according to the statistics – to live for a further 17.4 years, until she reached the ripe old age of 87.4 years old.

The funny thing about longevity (clearly there is nothing funny about death, so it is probably more quirky than funny) is that the older we get, the better our life expectancy gets. The same woman who could expect to live until 87.4 years old once she reached her 70th birthday would have a revised life expectancy of 90.6 years old on her 80th birthday. Thus, the older we get, the better our chances of living for a bit longer. Call it a 'survival bonus' if you like.

> The older we get, the better our chances of living for a bit longer.

Another implication of living longer

There are some other consequences to consider as a result of living just that bit longer.

The age profile of society has started to shift. Our nation, as a whole, is starting to get older. This means that there are more people in retirement and fewer people in work. There are now more people in the UK who are over 60 years old than there are people under the age of 16. The number of people over 85 years old has increased by over 500 per cent to 1.1 million since 1951.

> **The age profile of society has started to shift.**

The fact that there are fewer taxpayers means there is less money available to the State to support people in retirement. This increasing pressure to support an ageing population with fewer financial resources coming in from taxpayers could explain the Government's moves to increase the State pension age.

What this demographic shift also means is that more people in retirement still have living parents. Fifty years ago that was virtually unheard of. Today, it is not unusual for a retired couple to have at least one set of parents who are still alive.

The 60-year-old kid

Early retirement makes it even more likely that your parents will still be alive when you come to retire. You need to face the possibility that your parents may require financial assistance from you. A common example is elderly parents who require long-term care. Care fees can be astronomical and very little assistance is available from the State if you own property or any other assets.

This trend of people reaching retirement age with one or more parents still living has been dubbed in the US 'the 60-year-old kid'. At the start of the twentieth century, less than 7 per cent of people in their sixties still had a parent alive. This is now estimated to be around 49 per cent and rising.

Having living parents who may need financial assistance after you retire is not a good reason to postpone or cancel your plans for an early retirement. You should, however, consider the potential implications of this demographic shift for you and how this relates to their plans for retirement.

There is nothing average about you

It is great to talk about improved longevity, even when this poses some challenges for retirement and early retirement planning. Unfortunately, we can only ever talk about averages and you are not average! For retirement planning purposes, it makes more sense to assume that you will have a longer life expectancy than average. The risk of your money running out before you die is often greater than the cost of having too much money during your retirement.

> You are not average!

Fortunately, there is a financial instrument available that reduces this risk of living too long for your funds. An annuity is a way of providing a guaranteed income for life. We look at this option in more detail in Chapter 5. It will continue to pay a regular income regardless of how long you live. This is great news if you live past 100 years old, but the main drawback (in all senses of the word!) occurs if you die sooner than expected.

Life expectancy is an integral part of planning for an early retirement and can force you to make some tough decisions.

Getting ready for the early retirement plan

> The future belongs to those who prepare for it today.
>
> Malcolm X (1925–1965)

02

Preparation is an essential part of making the RTYE plan succeed. We all find things easier to achieve when we have a clear plan of action and understand what is needed to reach the end goal. This chapter is all about the preparation you will need to undertake to succeed with the RTYE plan.

In this chapter, we shall look at what it means to be organised and the benefits you will receive from making the effort to be a more organised person. We then take a look at the 'early retirement roadblocks' that can throw your plans to retire 10 years early off course.

Taking a look at bank statements can be a painful experience. Interpreting pension and investment statements is never easy. However, an important part of planning to implement the RTYE plan is understanding exactly where you are right now. Later in this chapter we shall look at how you can accurately assess your current financial position with minimal fuss and hassle.

Finally, we shall look at a few items that it is helpful to have in your RTYE toolkit. They are simple items that will make your progress with the RTYE plan much easier to monitor and manage. Think of this as your shopping list for an early retirement plan.

First, some good news

In the UK, we are better at getting ready for retirement than our European neighbours. The average age we are when we start to put money into a pension plan is 28 years old. This beats Germany, at 31 years old, Italy, at 32 years old, and Spain, at 34 years old.

The worst culprits in the world for starting their planning early appear to be the Japanese, who wait, on average, until they are 39 years old before putting money into a pension plan.

Our current average starting age for retirement planning is much better than the generation who have already retired. They, on average, didn't start putting money into a pension plan until they were 35 years old.

This head start on retirement planning really counts. Some research conducted by Fidelity International (Retirement Savings Research, 26 June 2006) found that every pound paid into a pension fund at the age of 25 has a potential retirement value of £7.88. Compare this with every pound paid into a pension at age 40, when the potential retirement value is just £3.37.

All is not lost for those who do not start their retirement planning in their 20s or early 30s. If you decide to take control of your plans for an early retirement at a later age, you can still make a substantial difference to your financial position and lifestyle in retirement.

The best chances of an early retirement come to those who start planning early. This head start makes the goal of retiring 10 years early easier to achieve and considerably cheaper. It's not impossible to retire 10 years early once you get into your 40s or 50s, but you will need a big dose of determination and focus to make it happen.

> The best chances of an early retirement come to those who start planning early.

Getting organised

I might not be the best person to lecture on this subject. My organisational skills vary wildly depending on the pressure of my workload.

When I get a quieter period (note the quieter – it's never actually *quiet* in my line of work), I use the additional time to get myself extremely well organised. Piles of paper that have been gradually growing over previous months are sorted through. Areas of my desk that went missing in the distant past become reacquainted with daylight. It's a positive experience and one that I tend to repeat a couple of times a year.

For the majority of the year, however, I work in a less than perfectly organised state. I thrive on organised chaos and take the view that, as long as I know where things can be found, that's OK.

I might try to kid myself that there is no problem with this view, but I know the truth is different. When I am better organised, I do find that it is less stressful and I get a lot more done. The same applies to early retirement planning.

If you are well organised, then your journey to early retirement will be far less stressful than would be the case otherwise. You will also find it easier to monitor your progress and take corrective action when required. It will be a far more pleasant journey.

Getting organised requires commitment and you have to set aside a sufficient amount of time to make it happen. Starting to try and get better organised is destined to result in failure if you go into the exercise without total commitment.

> **Getting organised requires commitment.**

Clare Evans is a personal and business coach (www.clareevans.co.uk). Clare says:

When you start thinking about your retirement (the sooner you start the better), planning your time is the best way to ensure you make the most of the time you have. Planning what you need to do at the beginning of each year, each month and each week is essential and will help to keep you on track. If you don't know where you're going, how will you know when you've got there?

Just a few minutes at the beginning or end of each day can make a huge difference to how productive you'll be. Break things down into steps and actions that you can achieve each day or each week. Arrange time in your diary for these tasks, whether it's dealing with e-mails, making phone calls or doing some research, not just for your appointments and meetings.

Early retirement roadblocks

There are a number of factors that can get in the way of the RTYE plan. I call these 'early retirement roadblocks'. Some of these roadblocks can completely destroy your plans to retire 10 years early. Other roadblocks are a mere annoyance that might distract you from your main objective.

When combined, these roadblocks can (and do) bring your RTYE plan to a grinding halt.

To clear these roadblocks from your path, you need to identify them and then deal with them. Knowing what your personal RTYE roadblocks look and feel like will ensure that you are better prepared to sweep them to one side.

Roadblock 1: Your partner

Retiring 10 years early is often easier if you are single. This is not solely the result of not having a partner and family to support, but because you can make decisions without having to make your strategy also fit with that of your partner.

Some recent research in America suggests that one third of couples disagree on the sort of lifestyle they will live during retirement (Richard W. Johnson, 'Do spouses coordinate their retirement decisions?', Center for Retirement Research, Boston College, July 2004). Over one third disagree on something as simple as their target retirement date. On top of this, around two in five of those surveyed cannot even agree about who will work during retirement.

If you are part of a couple, then this is the first and most important roadblock to address. Sweeping this roadblock to one side is all about communication. Retirement planning is likely to fail until both of you agree on the various objectives and then work together as a team to make these happen.

Men and women seem to have different goals when it comes to early retirement. A study by AXA found that only a third of women want to retire early compared to over half of men (AXA Retirement Scope 2007, 'Retirement Dreams and Realities'). Only 40 per cent of women would give up their job tomorrow, given the chance, compared to 50 per cent of men.

The same study did find some unity between the sexes when it came to the ideal age for retirement. Both men and women thought that the mid-50s were the perfect years to retire.

Until you can both see eye-to-eye on your joint plans for retirement you will be wasting a lot of energy working towards different objectives. This energy is better spent on working towards the same goal.

Talk to your partner and discover his or her expectations for retirement. Tell your partner about your own expectations. Make sure that they match. If they don't match, then

> Agree on joint goals before setting off on your RTYE plan.

compromise and agree on joint goals before setting off on your RTYE plan.

Roadblock 2: Inflation

Goods and services become more expensive over time. A loaf of bread cost around 9p in 1970, but will now set you back around £1. It will cost more than this in 10 years' time and significantly more than this in 50 years' time. Apply this trend of increasing prices to all of the goods and services you buy and it is easy to see why it becomes a potential roadblock.

Because retirement is lasting longer than ever before, the impact of price inflation is more serious. Retiring 10 years early will mean that there are an extra 10 years of retirement for the pressure of price inflation to really hurt your bank balance.

Added to this is the fact that inflation is typically higher for older people – around 30 per cent higher for someone aged over 75. This means that the headline inflation figure published by the Government each month should be taken with a pinch of salt by retired people.

> The headline inflation figure should be taken with a pinch of salt by retired people.

The way to sweep away this roadblock is to know about it and plan for it. If you take a higher rate of inflation into account when working out how your income needs to increase during retirement, you should be able to keep pace with the rising cost of living.

Later in the book we will take a look at some of the pension and investment vehicles you can use to plan for an early retirement. These include pension annuities, which provide a guaranteed income for life, regardless of how long you live. Choosing the right sort of pension annuity that will take this price inflation factor into account is essential.

Roadblock 3: Divorce

The financial implications of a divorce can be devastating for both the husband and wife. Getting divorced involves much more than just sharing joint assets between two people. It also means extensive legal costs, additional expenses to rebuild your life and loss of earnings during and after the divorce process.

In my role as an independent financial adviser, I work out the financial aspects of divorce on a regular basis. The couples involved vary from those with modest assets and incomes to the ultra-wealthy. None of them can honestly say that they have ended up in a superior financial position as a result of divorce (even with my expert help and guidance!).

Steering clear of this roadblock is tough because divorce very often hits those who least expect it. My counsel is to do everything you can to minimise the financial impact of divorce if it strikes you in the future. Seek professional advice, not just from a family lawyer but also a financial planner and divorce counsellor. Some of the worst financial agreements I have seen occur when the divorcing couple fails to consult a professional financial planner.

Reaching an amicable agreement quickly and in a cost-effective manner has to be preferable to a long and bitter confrontation in the courts. Collaborative law is starting to make a big splash in the UK as a more amicable approach to resolving conflict during divorce.

Do what you can to enable you to put the divorce behind you quickly and refocus on your financial objectives.

Roadblock 4: Debt

Debt is a drag on your ability to meet your financial objectives. As you will see in Chapter 4, debt destruction is a very important part of the RTYE plan.

> Debt destruction is a very important part of the RTYE plan.

Debt is more than just an expensive drag on your resources, though. It is also a symptom of bad financial management and lack of self-control.

When we want to buy anything, we all have a choice. We can either buy it now or buy it when we can afford it. Buying something now without the cash available to do so will mean taking on debt. Waiting until we can afford to buy the item actually makes it cheaper because we will benefit from interest on our savings and have no interest to pay on any debt!

If you make one decision today, decide to stop taking on unsecured debt and start to rid yourself of any existing debt you have. If you can control your debt, then you stand a good chance of succeeding with the RTYE plan.

Roadblock 5: You

Each of the above roadblocks can pose a serious threat to the RTYE plan. Some are more serious than others. Combined they can be deadly. This final roadblock, however, is the most serious of them all.

If you decide that you cannot retire 10 years early, then you will have created an early retirement roadblock that cannot be passed.

> **Your attitude needs to be fully aligned with your financial objectives.**

Your attitude needs to be fully aligned with your financial objectives for retirement before you embark on the RTYE plan. Having the wrong attitude will result in you having to work for longer and wait until much later in life before you can enjoy retirement.

We can achieve almost anything, within reason, that we put our minds to. Being determined to retire 10 years early and having that as a clear goal is not unreasonable. Once you have decided it is what you want, and you put every effort into making it a reality, it will become a reality very quickly.

The perils of parents

Your plans for an early retirement can be thrown off course by a number of factors. During the build-up phase of your early retirement plans, it is likely to be your children that give rise to the biggest financial expenses. Once you have actually retired, it can often be your parents.

Because we are all living for longer, it is no longer unusual for your parents to still be alive once you have retired. You drastically increase the chances of this being the case if you choose to retire 10 years early. Living for longer often leads to poor health in old age. As we get older, the chances of requiring long-term care increase. Care can be required in the family home or at a residential or nursing home. Before your parents reach their 70s or 80s, you need to have a strategy in place for protecting your wealth and their best interests if they become unwell.

The best way to reduce the risk of your parents having a serious impact on your plans for retirement is to talk to them. It is often difficult to talk about money with your parents. The older generation tends to be quite secretive when it comes to talking about their finances. There is also a danger that they will think you are sniffing around about your inheritance!

If you find it difficult to have this sort of discussion with your parents, at least encourage them to talk to your financial adviser. If your financial adviser can provide advice to different generations of your family, he or she will stand a good chance of understanding the bigger picture.

You should also involve any brothers or sisters you have in this process. By working together as a team, you can tackle future planning issues together to find the best solution. Getting financial assistance from more members of the family also means that it spreads any costs you might have to incur in the future.

Where are you right now?

The most important thing you can do to get ready for the RTYE plan is work out where you are, financially, right now. This task is easier for some people than others.

If you have adopted the 'ostrich approach' to personal finance up until now, it might require a lot of effort to assess your current

Getting over the fear of seeing your bank statement is an important step.

financial position. This is because you are unlikely to (a) know exactly what you have and (b) want to know!

Getting over the fear of seeing your bank statement is an important step for a lot of people. I always look at this as being a bit like removing a plaster. If you do it quickly, it won't hurt that much. Reveal the sorry state of your personal finances slowly and it will be a painful, drawn-out experience.

If you are well organised when it comes to your money, then this task will be easy. You can probably skip this stage and move on to the more important bits coming up later in the chapter. Alternatively, you might want to keep reading to make sure that what you already know about your money matches what you need to know to start taking control.

The information you will need

There are only four bits of information you really need to prepare for the RTYE plan:

- income
- expenditure
- assets
- liabilities.

Sounds pretty simple? Watch out, though, as the devil is, as they say, in the detail. Let's take a closer look at each of these four items to make sure that you have everything you need.

Income

There are two numbers that you need to understand here. The

first is your 'gross' income – the headline salary and bonuses you get paid each year. The second is your 'net' income – the money that actually makes it into your bank account each month after the deduction of tax.

You also need to make a prediction about how fast your income will grow in the future. You can do this in one of two ways.

- You can look up the National Average Earnings (NAE) figure, which is a measurement of how fast earnings in the UK grow each year. This figure is only an average, so there is no certainty that your earnings will keep pace with this – they could grow faster or slower than the average figure.

- The alternative is to look at the pay increases you have received in the past. This is likely to be a more accurate prediction of the future if you have been in your job for a reasonable period of time – say, five years or more. Bear in mind that your earning power tends to improve as you get older and gain experience. You should expect your income to increase at a faster pace the older you get.

For the purpose of this exercise, you should ignore any irregular income, such as gifts from family members, sale proceeds from a property or inheritance. These are likely to be one-off events, so will not be part of a regular and reliable stream of income in the future.

Expenditure

You need to know what leaves your bank account each month. There are two types of expenditure to make a note of – fixed and discretionary.

- Your *fixed* expenditure is the amount of money you have to spend each month. You need to include in this things like your mortgage payments, utility bills, other debt repayment and food bills.

■ Your *discretionary* expenditure is loosely covered by the term 'fun stuff'. It's the stuff that you might not want to stop spending money on but could live without.

The easy test as to whether something falls into the fixed or discretionary expenditure camp is to think about what would happen if you stopped spending money on that item for a month or longer.

If something falls into the category of fixed expenditure, then it is likely that something bad would happen if you stopped spending your money on it. You would get a nasty letter (if it was your mortgage) or starve to death (if it was your food bill), say.

If something is discretionary expenditure, it would be annoying to stop spending your money on it, but not the end of the world.

It is really important to be clear about which items of expenditure are fixed and which are discretionary – for reasons that will become very clear later in the book.

> It is important to be clear about which items of expenditure are fixed and which are discretionary.

To get an accurate idea of your expenditure, you should look back over three years' worth of bank statements. If you pay for lots of things using cheques, then you will need the old cheque stubs to match up the transactions.

For the purpose of this exercise, you should ignore any money you have put into savings. This is a form of expenditure, as it is money leaving your bank account, but the money still belongs to you so you don't need to count it as true expenditure.

Assets

Your assets are the things you own. This can include almost anything that you are the legal owner of, but, once again, you need to separate your assets into two categories.

- Your liquid assets. 'Liquid' in this sense means stuff that you can easily convert to hard cash. In this category are cash (not surprisingly!) and other investments. Anything that you can sell easily at short notice can be classed as a liquid asset.

- Your non-liquid assets. These are things that would take a longer period of time to sell or you could not convert to cash at all. Any property you own would normally be included in this category because of the time it takes to complete a property sale. You should also include any pension funds here because of the rules that prevent you from converting these to cash.

Be realistic about the value you place on each asset. Dinner party conversations about rising property prices are fine, but, in reality, the value of your house is what somebody else is willing to pay for it when you want to sell it. House price trends are not very accurate in predicting the value of an individual property.

> Be realistic about the value you place on each asset.

However, it has become easier in recent years to discover the likely value of your house because historical property sale data is readily available on the Internet. With some mild digital snooping, it is possible to find out exactly what Mr and Mrs Jones at number 24 sold their three-bed semi for last April. Also, if you find similar properties sold recently, you should be able to come up with a fairly accurate indication of the value of your own property.

Liabilities

This means the money that you owe to other people or institutions. You have probably guessed already that there are two different types of liabilities (a bit of a recurring theme in this chapter!).

- Secured debt. This is the debt that is linked to one of your assets, as described in the previous section. The best example of a secured debt is a mortgage. This is a financial liability linked to your property. When you take out a mortgage, the bank or other lender will usually have a first charge on your property. In simple terms this means that, if you can't afford to pay the mortgage, the lender has the right to take ownership of your property. It doesn't mean that the mortgage company owns your property under normal circumstances, but it does have the ability to take ownership if you cannot meet your liabilities.

- Unsecured debt. This is also known as personal debt or bad debt. It's a type of liability that isn't explicitly linked to an asset. The reality is that you might have taken on this type of debt to buy something specific, such as a television or a leather sofa. This doesn't make it secured debt as the liability rests squarely with you – the lender does not have a charge over your TV or sofa.

Be as accurate as possible when recording the details of these liabilities. This means checking an up-to-date statement from each lender. Make sure that you know the date when you took on the liability, how much you pay each month, what the interest rate is and when the liability will be repaid.

For your mortgage, it is also important to find out the payment basis (are you just paying the interest each month or are you repaying the capital as well?), if the interest rate can change and if there are any penalties for repaying part or your entire mortgage. Such penalties are known as redemption penalties.

Building your toolkit

Now you have got this far, you know the importance of getting organised, what potential roadblocks can get in your way and the numbers you have to understand before you implement the RTYE plan. The final part of getting ready for the RTYE plan is building a toolkit.

The following are some suggested items and services that will help you to make and monitor your progress with the RTYE plan.

The trick here is not to spend too much money on the items on this list. That would be a counterproductive move. Make use of things you already own or have access to. Where you do need to buy something to make up this toolkit, then shop around and pay a good price for it.

The folder

One of the most important parts of the RTYE toolkit is a ring binder. Go for a large lever arch-type ring binder rather than one of those flimsy small ones. Your RTYE folder is your key to keeping paperwork organised and accessible. As time goes by, you may need to buy more of these as your records expand. Use dividers to create different sections within the folder. Always file away paperwork as it arrives, assuming you have dealt with anything that needs to be dealt with.

Your RTYE folder should take pride of place on a bookshelf or in a cabinet in your house. Do not file and forget. It will contain everything relevant to your plans for an early retirement. You will need to refer to this folder on a regular basis, so do not hide it away somewhere to gather dust.

The Internet

Access to the Internet is essential for ongoing research. It will also make it easier (and cheaper) for you to invest money and monitor your progress. The majority of bank accounts now come with Internet banking, which enables you to view statements and move money around. Using the Internet to manage your finances saves a great deal of time that you would otherwise need to spend standing in queues. It is also possible to get better rates of interest on savings if you are prepared to use an Internet-based account.

> Access to the Internet is essential for ongoing research.

There is no need to go out and spend hundreds of pounds on a new computer to access the Internet from home. Such access is readily available in every town and city at Internet cafés. You can even get free Internet access in public libraries.

When viewing anything confidential on the Internet in a public place, you should make sure that you keep your data secure. Delete your browsing history before leaving the computer and make sure that nobody is paying too much attention to what you are doing on the computer.

Notebooks

You should always have a way of making notes close at hand. Ideas, inspiration and knowledge that will assist you with the RTYE plan can come to you at any time.

My favourite notebooks are from Moleskine – made famous by Van Gogh and Hemingway. They are so nice to look at that it is almost a shame to write in them! As an alternative for more general scribbling, I often use school notebooks, which are cheap, cheerful and effective. Apparently, the great entrepreneur Richard Branson is fond of using school notebooks.

Some of my best ideas come to me when I am out walking the dog. Instead of carrying a notebook with me, I take a small digital voice recorder to capture these ideas. This plugs straight into my computer when I get back from the walk so I can download my notes and type them up at a later date.

An independent financial adviser

The services of a good independent financial adviser are absolutely essential for your RTYE toolkit. You need to find somebody who can implement investments for you and provide a 'sanity check' for your plans. Depending on how involved you want to get with your financial planning, you may even want to pay a financial adviser to construct and review your plans on your behalf.

> Find somebody who can implement investments for you and provide a 'sanity check'.

It is vital that the financial adviser you choose is wholly independent. Using a tied or multi-tied financial adviser will not allow you to get best value for money – only independence can guarantee this in an ever-changing financial market.

You should tell your financial adviser about your plans for an early retirement and ask him or her where they can add value to these plans. Look for an adviser you can see yourself working with for a very long time. Ideally you should find an adviser who is a similar age to you to ensure that he or she does not retire before you!

Budgeting for an early retirement

> A budget is just a method of worrying before you spend money, as well as afterward.
>
> Anonymous

03

> **Get your budget right and the rest should follow.**

A well-designed and managed budget is the most important tool you have to support your RTYE plan. Forget about pension plans and investments for a moment because, if you get your budgeting wrong (or neglect to budget at all), none of your other financial plans will matter. Get your budget right and the rest should follow.

Budgeting is all about spending less than you earn. Effective budgeting is essential because it will allow you to save money now that can be put towards your early retirement plans. It will also give you a clear idea of how much money you will need during retirement to maintain your standard of living.

If you do not currently work to a budget, then this chapter will help you establish this important building block. Your budget is the blueprint for building your financial plan.

If you do already have a budget in place and you consistently manage to stick to it, then you will still find important information in this chapter about how to use your budget to plan for your early retirement.

The benefits of budgeting

Apart from the obvious benefit of ensuring that you plan to spend less than you earn, there are a number of other benefits associated with budgeting.

Drawing up a budget and sticking to it will help you avoid debt. The next chapter looks at debt in more detail, but, needless to say, it is expensive and a real drag on your ability to meet your financial objectives. If you keep falling into the debt trap, you will find it difficult, if not impossible, to retire 10 years early.

Having a budget makes it easier to make decisions about what you buy and spend your money on. This might sound like it takes the fun out of browsing the High Street, but it is an important discipline to learn if you are to stand any chance of early retirement.

It also adds a sense of realism to your early retirement plans. Without a budget it is difficult to establish whether or not the RTYE plan will be possible.

Some rules

There are some important rules to follow when creating and sticking to your budget. If you can manage to stick to these rules, then you will be on the right track for financial success. Failure to stick to these rules will make having a budget a miserable experience that you quickly try to forget.

> Stick to these rules, then you will be on the right track for financial success.

1 **Never underestimate items of expenditure.** If you are not sure of the exact cost of a particular item of expenditure, then it is always better to overestimate. This might make your budget look more expensive, but at least it will mean you have extra money left over at the end of the month if your estimate was wrong. A precise figure in your budget is always better than a guess, but a high guess is always better than a low guess.

2 **Don't budget to spend every last penny.** The worst budget is a tight budget. When I was younger, I tried to live on a tight budget for a while. It didn't work for long. I scraped by for a few months and then some unexpected expenditure did serious damage to my finances. You need to leave a healthy amount of breathing space in your budget if you want it to succeed in the long term. If this spare capacity isn't spent on things you didn't anticipate, then it simply means you have more money that can go towards your plan for early retirement. If you do end up being forced to spend the spare part of your budget, at least you didn't go into the red.

3 **Don't view the expenditure items within your budget as minimum spends.** Think of these items as being a bit like the speed limit for driving. There is no law that says you have to drive at the speed limit, but you will be punished if you drive faster. The items of expenditure in your budget are not there to force you to spend that money each month, but are there to make you aware of the spending that is likely to crop up. Treat them as such.

4 **Once you have written your budget, check it carefully and keep it under review.** Alongside each item of expenditure, you should have another column in which to record what you *actually* spent. Review your budget at the end of each month and see how accurate your spending predictions were. If you find that you are spending more or less than expected, do not rush to make changes to your budget. Make a note of any differences, but wait at least three months before you alter the numbers in your budget. They may just be one-offs or they may reflect a longer-term trend. By waiting for three months, you can see if you are consistently spending more or less than expected.

Signs of bad budgeting

If any of the following apply to you, then you need to take a closer look at your budgeting. These should all be considered as a prompt to sit down with your budget and take a hard look at each item of expenditure. Until you get your budget back under control, making progress with the RTYE plan will be next to impossible.

1 **You don't pay off your credit card in full each month.** There is nothing wrong with using a credit card to buy things. In fact, for certain purchases, it can even give you an added degree of consumer protection. There *is* something wrong with not paying your card off, in full, each and every month. It means two things. First, you are spending more than you earn each month and your budget has failed. Second, you have to pay extra for the items you are buying on your credit card in the form of interest. These are both strong indications of a poor budget or lack of willpower to stick to your budget.

2 **You start getting desperate for more money towards the end of the month.** If your budget is working correctly, then pay day should come and go without much of a fuss. It is a sign of a poor budget if the last few days of each month are marked by you scrabbling around behind the sofa searching for loose change. Your budget should ensure that you spread your income and expenditure evenly over the whole month. Blowing your salary in the first three weeks and then living like a hermit for the final part of the month is not a good way to budget.

3 **Using your emergency fund when it isn't an emergency.** Having an emergency fund – cash savings designed to see you through times of trouble – is a good financial practice. Once you manage to build up an emergency fund – which should contain between three and six months' typical expenditure – you have to save it for emergencies. If you find yourself

frequently dipping into the emergency fund and then having to replenish it over the next few months, something is not going well with your budgeting.

4 **Fighting about money with your spouse or partner.** Money can be the source of arguments and stress. Partners will sometimes disagree about the best use of the money they have available. If you find yourself involved in these disagreements about money on a regular basis, then you may need to re-address your budget. Budgeting when you have a spouse or partner who shares income and expenditure has to be a joint activity. There is nothing wrong with one partner taking responsibility for the budget, but both of you need to be singing from the same hymn sheet. Something else that falls into this broad category is buying things and then not being completely truthful with your partner. This might involve not telling him or her about the purchase at all or being 'creative' about the cost. If you find yourself in the position of having to lie about what you have spent money on, then you need to review your budget and the reasons for having it in place.

5 **Altering your budget on a regular basis.** If you find yourself changing the numbers in your budget more than twice a year, it means one of two things. It could mean that your original estimates were way off track. If this is the case, you should learn your lesson and make sure that your revised numbers are more accurate. However, it is more likely to mean that you are not managing to stick to the original budget and the only way to make the numbers work is to change them. If you find yourself doing this, then you need to stop and think back to why you have the budget in place and stick to it. Keeping to a budget is the best way to ensure that you meet your main objective of early retirement. Chopping and changing the numbers when it suits you will reduce the chances of it ever happening.

Some assumptions

When you are budgeting and using this as a basis for your early retirement plans, you will need to make several assumptions about the future. These assumptions will help you to understand how your budget is likely to change over time and what additional steps you need to take to plan for your early retirement.

> **Assumptions change.**

Keep in mind that assumptions change. If you make an assumption today and then forget about it for 20 years, there is little chance that it will have been correct. When you make any assumptions for your budgeting or early retirement planning, you must review them regularly. By reviewing your assumptions on an annual basis you will have the opportunity to establish how accurate they were. It will also allow you to make changes to your budget and other financial plans to take into account any changes to your assumptions. This is easily done if the incorrect assumption is identified regularly. It is much harder to take corrective action if you wait for a long time before realising that it is necessary.

> **Review them regularly.**

There are four main assumptions that you need to keep in mind when constructing your plans for an early retirement.

1 **Price inflation.** This is the measure of how quickly the goods
and services we buy are becoming more expensive. The most
commonly used measure of price inflation is the Retail Prices
Index (RPI). The Government has been regularly updating
this index since 1947. The rate of price inflation has varied
wildly over the years. Back in the mid 1970s it reached a peak
of 24 per cent a year. This means that a loaf of bread costing
you 50p at the start of the year would have cost you around
62p at the end of that year. As I write, the level of price inflation seems fairly settled, at around 3 per cent a year. The
Government has a lower long-term inflation target so it
should be safe to assume a price inflation rate of 2.5 per cent
a year for your early retirement plans.

2 **Earnings inflation.** The cost of living increases each year, but,
fortunately, our earnings tend to go up as well! If they didn't,
then we would all find it much harder to make ends meet
each month. Earnings inflation is normally measured by the
National Average Earnings (NAE) index. Earnings tend to
increase at a faster rate than price inflation. Historically, earnings have outpaced price inflation by around 1.5 to 2.5 per
cent a year over the long term. So, if you assume a price inflation figure of 2.5 per cent a year, you might assume that your
earnings will grow each year by around 4 per cent.

3 **Investment growth.** When you invest your money, you expect
it to grow. We all know that investments can go down in
value as well as up, but, over the long term, it would be reasonable to expect most investments to go up in value. In
Chapter 6, we explain how the level of risk you take with
your investments will dictate the potential return. When you
make an assumption about future investment growth, you
need to keep this under regular review so you can readjust
your assumptions on an annual basis to ensure that they are
accurate. Many financial products and investments will come
with an illustration that contains a projection. This

projection tends to assume three different investment growth rates – the lower rate of 5 per cent a year, the middle rate of 7 per cent a year and a higher rate of 9 per cent a year. These growth rates are never guaranteed and you should not think of them as lower or higher limits on your investments. They are chosen as a way of consistently comparing the charges on different financial products and investments. If the assumed growth rates are all the same, then the difference in the final projected fund value after, say, 10 years is down to the charges levied on the investment. A lower projected fund means higher charges.

4 **Mortality.** We took a detailed look at life expectancy and longevity in Chapter 1. For the purpose of budgeting and financial planning, it is important to consider how long you are likely to live, but it is also rather irrelevant. The average life expectancy is not much use when trying to work out how long your money has to last because you might not be very average! For planning purposes, you might want to assume that you will live to 99 years old. Even in a society where life expectancy seems to be getting better all of the time, 99 years old is still something of an achievement. If you base your mortality assumptions on living to 99, then you stand a good chance of working towards having enough wealth in place to sustain your lifestyle during retirement. If you die earlier than 99 years old, you can leave money to your children or other beneficiaries. If you live longer than 99 years old, then at least you'll get a telegram from the Queen!

What next?

Once you have drawn up a budget and managed to stick to it consistently for a few months, it's time to get creative. To be in a financial position to retire 10 years early, you will need to direct more of your income towards achieving this goal.

> **It's time to get creative.**

Take a detailed look at every single item of expenditure and consider how you can cut it down or remove it altogether. In Chapter 7 we will look at a number of ways to slash your costs and cut down on your total outgoings. This part of the plan has to be radical and it will involve you making some tough choices.

> **This part of the plan has to be radical and will involve making some tough choices.**

Financial planning often comes down to a question of priorities. Because most of us have limited financial resources, we can only afford to meet a limited number of financial objectives. Succeeding with your plans for an early retirement could mean making the choice between spending today and retiring earlier.

Spending money when you have retired

To be able to plan to retire 10 years early, you need to know four things about your expenditure when you retire.

- What bills stop?
- What bills reduce?
- What bills remain the same?
- What bills will increase?

Let's take a look at each of these in turn to see if we can identify where your different items of expenditure are likely to be categorised.

Bills that stop

From a planning perspective, this is the category that frees up more of your income. It also reduces the need for you to put aside as much of your money in the run-up to retirement. It is a good category for expenditure items to fall into. Unfortunately, relatively few items of expenditure are likely to completely stop when you retire.

While these items of expenditure are few and far between, they do include what for many people is the single largest cost each month – the mortgage. Most mortgages are set up so that they are fully repaid by the time you retire. It is unusual, although not completely unheard of, for a mortgage to run past your normal retirement age.

However, if you plan to retire 10 years early, you need to give some thought to your mortgage. In the next chapter you will learn the importance of debt destruction. This includes repaying your mortgage at a faster pace than you are currently. Making these overpayments should reduce your mortgage term, but you will need to ensure that the new term coincides with your plans for earlier retirement.

The other big cost saving in retirement is children. By the time most people traditionally retire, their children have finished in full-time education and, hopefully, started to pay their own way in life. However, early retirement can create a clash with continued expenditure on your children. For one or more children to still be at university when their parents are 65 years old is unusual. There is a greater chance that they will still be at university studying (and drinking!) when their parents are 55 years old or younger.

Other outgoings that stop when you retire are National Insurance contributions. These are only compulsory when you are working if you are younger than 60 (for a woman) and 65 (for a man). You can continue to make voluntary National Insurance contributions and, if you are a man, you automatically receive credits if you are not working between the ages of 60 and 65. It can be helpful to pay voluntary National Insurance contributions if you are not working or your income is too low to cause you to make contributions under the ordinary system. This will ensure that you fill any gaps in your National Insurance contribution record and are entitled to a full State Pension when you reach pensionable age.

Bills that reduce

Expenses related to employment are the ones that commonly fall after retirement. This will, of course, depend on your decision to continue to work or fully retire. If you do fully retire from work, then the costs associated with clothing for work and commuting will both be lower than they were during your working life. You will continue to spend money on both clothes and travel, but this expenditure is likely to be significantly lower than it used to be.

Bills that remain the same

The bad news is that you will continue to spend money during retirement on the vast majority of things you spend money on today. Take a look down the list of expenditure items in your budget and identify the things that you will still need to include when you retire.

In fact, these items will not actually stay the same. They will increase in line with price inflation.

Bills that increase

Items of expenditure that fall into this final category are often down to your personal lifestyle and the choices you make during retirement. Leisure and travel expenditure commonly increases during retirement as people have more free time to indulge themselves in the activities that they have always wanted to do.

> Everything you spend money on during retirement will increase.

In fact, everything you spend money on during retirement will increase. This is because goods and services become more expensive over time. Price inflation is actually worse for people who have retired than people who are still in work. The head-line rate of price inflation that is published by the Government each month hides this fact.

Price inflation increases at a faster rate for older people because the items they spend more of their money on tend to go up in price at a faster rate than other things. Some analysis of annual expenditure figures suggests that the cost of living for the over-75s is 56 per cent higher than that for the rest of the population (Prudential, 'Cost of living for retired people rising faster than national average', 25 July 2007). This means that there is a significant increase in the cost of living as you get older.

How to manage your budget

My parents tell me that, when they were my age, they used to manage their budget with envelopes. They would keep a series of envelopes and each one would relate to a different item of expenditure. This strategy sounds to me like a very neat (if a bit unsafe!) way of keeping track of your budgeting.

My wife and I use a slightly different budgeting technique that relies on two things. First, we have a number of different savings accounts that serve different purposes. These include an account to pay the tax bill and another account for save for holidays. It doesn't cost us anything extra to have a number of different savings accounts. With Internet banking, it is simple to move money from these accounts to our current account when needed.

Second, we draw enough cash at the start of each week to pay for things such as food and transport. That way we reduce the temptation to use debit or credit cards to pay for things. Knowing that you have to make a certain amount of cash last for the entire week is a powerful motivator to stay on track.

These might not be the most sophisticated of systems, but they are highly effective. The important thing about having systems like these is putting some thought into them. The existence of such budgeting systems is more important than the actual system you decide to use. Just having a budgeting system will greatly increase your chances of sticking to your budget.

The best budgets are those that are realistic, written down and regularly reviewed.

> Having a budgeting system will greatly increase your chances of sticking to your budget.

Debt destruction

> We pay our debts to the past by putting the future in debt to ourselves.
>
> John Buchan (1875–1940)

04

Debt is a drag. It's a drag on your ability to meet your financial objectives. For many people, debt is a constant source of worry and stress.

This chapter is all about debt destruction. I will tell and show you why paying off your mortgage early is one of the most effective uses of your financial resources when you are following the RTYE plan.

Why is debt a problem?

Rates of personal insolvency (the thing that happens when debt takes over completely) have been on the rise in the UK for years. As a nation, we have a pretty unhealthy relationship with debt. You only have to stay at home and watch some television during the day to understand the extent of the problem – you will see advert after advert of credit card offers and debt consolidation services. Daytime television viewers are a prime target for this sort of advertising.

However, the advertisements never show the consequences of debt. The companies love to show you that their latest balance transfer credit card offer can reduce your monthly outgoings and send you on that lovely holiday. I've yet to see an advert finish by explaining the months or years you will then have to sacrifice to pay for not only that fortnight on the beach but also the cost of interest on the debt you've incurred.

> The advertisements never show the consequences of debt.

I've said for a long time that credit cards should be renamed 'debt cards'. Maybe a vigorous rebranding exercise along these lines would encourage us to be a bit more careful about our spending and borrowing. That would be no good for the banks and other lenders that rake in billions of pounds each and every year because people cannot control their financial urges, though, so I can't see it happening.

When a large portion of your income each month is swallowed up by the cost of servicing debt, you are immediately on the back foot and financial survival for the rest of the month becomes a serious challenge. Yet, sorting out your relationship with debt is an essential part of the RTYE plan. People who beat their debt demons tend to have a healthier relationship with money and feel better off as a result than those who spend now and definitely pay later.

> **People who beat their debt demons tend to have a healthier relationship with money.**

Two types of debt

There are two types of debt – good and bad.

Good debt

Good debt is the debt created when you buy something that is likely to go up in value. For it to be classed as good debt, the thing you buy has to have the potential to go up in value at a faster pace than the cost of the debt. This means that, if the interest rate on the debt is 10 per cent each year, your asset (the thing you bought with that debt) needs to go up by 11 per cent each year, but preferably more.

It's called good debt because it serves a purpose and should result in you being wealthier in the long term.

> **The commonest form of good debt is a mortgage.**

The commonest form of good debt is a mortgage. This is, after all, just a really big loan – possibly the biggest loan you will ever have in your life. You use a mortgage to buy a property in the expectation that the property will go up in value at a faster rate than the cost of having the mortgage.

Bad debt

Bad debt is, as the name suggests, bad! It is the debt created when you buy things that will go down in value. Sometimes we create bad debt to buy things that have little value or no value at all. That holiday in Greece you bought using your credit card might have had a value at the point of purchase, but that value quickly disappears. The value usually disappears faster than your suntan.

> **The commonest forms of bad debt are credit cards and personal loans.**

The commonest forms of bad debt are credit cards and personal loans. The commonest type of really bad debt is store cards. They should come with a wealth warning. Not only do we use them to buy things that will fall in value, but they also prevent us from shopping around for the best deal – a double whammy of negative force on our finances.

Debt in retirement
Before we talk about ridding your life of bad (and good) debt

forever, let's spend a few moments thinking about the consequences of never getting rid of your bad debt.

Key Retirement Solutions carried out some research and found that 63 per cent of people over 60 years old still had bad debt ('Are UK pensioners heading towards a £98 billion mortgage debt time-bomb in retirement', 23 March 2007). The average credit card debt is over £7500 per pensioner. As a group, British pensioners owe around £25 billion on their credit cards. This excludes the additional bad debt many are servicing on their personal loans and overdrafts.

> **British pensioners owe around £25 billion on their credit cards.**

The story gets worse as pensioners get older. Those over 70 in this study had an average bad debt of a whopping £70,000 each! This meant average monthly payments of £450 each – a challenge when you are employed and earning a salary; a monumental feat when you are living on a small pension income.

When you plan ahead for your retirement, the last thing you want to still have is bad debt. Not only will this slow down your progress on the way to an early retirement, but it will also mean that you have to stretch your limited income in retirement to cover the cost of servicing your bad debt. When you barely have enough money in the kitty to pay the Council Tax and buy food, you do not want a credit card statement arriving on the doormat each month as well.

The first steps

Before embarking on the RTYE plan, you have to get your bad debt under control. In my first book, *The Money Tree* (Pearson Prentice Hall, 2006), I explained my five-step strategy for destroying debt. Here it is again, updated for the RTYE plan.

> " You have to get your bad debt under control.

1 **Stop making it worse.** Don't even think about getting started with the RTYE plan unless you can control yourself and stop taking on more bad debt. This doesn't necessarily mean cutting up your credit cards, but it does mean making a decision about your financial priorities and then sticking to that decision. If you keep building up bad debt, your early retirement plans will take longer to achieve and you may even never achieve early retirement at all.

> " Control yourself and stop taking on more bad debt.

2 **Decide first, then get on with it.** Destroying bad debt is tough. It is far easier to take on bad debt than it is to pay it off. Only start destroying your debt if you have every intention of sticking to this mission until all of the bad debt is gone. Think about what your life will be like without bad debt and how much easier it will be to reach your goals for an early retirement. Create a strong mental picture of this outcome and it will be easier to achieve.

3 Know your enemy. In Chapter 2, we looked at the financial information you need to collate before you start your RTYE plan. Destroying bad debt requires a similar level of information. Quantify your current bad debt position and write it down. This will be your main source of reference as you start to destroy your bad debt.

4 Make your plan of attack. Work out the best way to destroy your bad debt. It usually makes sense to start by paying off the bad debt that has the highest rate of interest, even if it does not represent your biggest debt. Set yourself regular milestones – this will make it easier to stay on track than just looking ahead to longer-term objectives.

> Set yourself regular milestones – this will make it easier to stay on track.

5 Allocate your resources. Regardless of our income and expenditure, we all have limited financial resources. Once you have established the scale of your bad debt and your plan of attack, you can work out how to put these limited resources to work. The money you use to clear your bad debt has to come from one of two places – spare income or savings. Both are equally important when it comes to destroying your bad debts, so put them to work and make them count.

Your mortgage

If you are anything like me, you will have a mortgage. This is my single largest item of expenditure each month. The time to pay for my mortgage comes around each month like clockwork and takes a huge chunk out of my income. My mortgage is, hopefully, the largest debt I will ever have in my life.

As house prices continue to climb, the mortgages we take out also increase. Whereas a 25-year mortgage used to be considered normal, it is not unusual to see people taking on mortgages for 30 or even 40 years. There is even a mortgage available that you can pass on to your children when you die – not the sort of inheritance you would want to receive!

The reason I work so hard is to cover the cost of my mortgage. If my mortgage was completely repaid tomorrow morning, I could happily reduce my working effort by around 30 per cent and the subsequent drop in income would be totally manageable.

Alternatively, I could continue working just as hard to see an immediate increase in my available income. This extra cash could then go towards helping me meet my other financial objectives, including an earlier retirement.

Given the chance to get rid of your mortgage tomorrow, what would you do? Would you work less and earn less or continue to work just as hard and put the money towards an early retirement?

They serve a purpose

It's easy to talk about the cost of a mortgage and ignore the purpose of having this debt in the first place. We take out mortgages to buy property. They serve a very important purpose as the vast majority of people could not afford to buy property at an early stage in their lives simply by saving hard and paying in cash.

The ability to borrow a substantial sum of money from a bank or other financial institution is what gets us on the property ladder when we buy our first homes. As our careers progress, we earn more and realise we can afford a bigger mortgage so move into a bigger home.

Mortgage mistakes

In a moment, we will consider why repaying your mortgage is such as important part of your RTYE plan and the ways you can reduce this debt faster. Before we do that, here are five of the commonest mortgage mistakes we see on a frequent basis when working with our clients.

1 Working with a small deposit. It pays to save hard and put down a big deposit when you buy a home. The more you can afford to put towards the purchase of your home from your own pocket, the better. This reduces the 'loan to value' (LTV) and gives you a couple of important benefits.

■ It offers you some protection if there is a drop in the property market. A bigger deposit means that, if the value of your home starts to fall, it should still be worth more than the outstanding mortgage. If your home is valued at less than your mortgage, you are in an unenviable position known as negative equity. This can be a serious problem when you decide to sell your home and the sale proceeds are insufficient to repay the mortgage. A bigger deposit means more protection from negative equity.

■ Having a bigger deposit will give you access to a better mortgage deal. Lenders like borrowers who have bigger deposits – it shows a bit of commitment and reduces the perceived risk of lending you hundreds of thousands of pounds. As a result, they reserve the best products and interest rates for borrowers with 5, 10 or 15 per cent deposits available. Saving for a bigger deposit really does pay.

Saving for a bigger deposit really does pay.

2 **Fixing and forgetting.** Fixed-rate mortgages can be very good. They give you a great deal of certainty that your monthly repayments will stay the same regardless of what is happening to the Bank of England's interest rate. Interest rates could be going through the roof and your mortgage would continue to cost you the same as when you started it. When the fixed rate period comes to an end, your mortgage reverts back to the lender's standard variable rate. If interest rates have been going up the whole time you have been on the fixed rate, then this day might come as a very nasty surprise. So, if you go for a fixed rate – and there is no reason not to – keep a close eye on what is likely to happen at the end of that fixed rate period.

3 **Extending terms.** People will typically start their mortgage with a 25-year term. Two years later, when it is time to reassess the market and consider a remortgage, an increasing number of people have a 25-year term for that one also. This creates the never-ending mortgage. Instead of resetting the term every time you remortgage, you should always stick to the original end date of your first mortgage. Write the date when your mortgage will come to an end in your diary and apply that end date to every mortgage you have in the future so the term keeps on reducing.

4 **Sticking with the standard variable rate.** The biggest mistake people make with their mortgage is paying the lender's standard variable rate. Think of this as the interest rate for lazy people. There are always better deals available if you are prepared to be a 'rate tart' and do some shopping around.

Be a 'rate tart' and do some shopping around.

5 Shopping around based on the headline interest rate. If you make mortgage decisions based only on the interest rate on offer, you are unlikely to get the best deal. What is more important is the *total* cost of the mortgage over a given time period. This total cost includes things such as the arrangement fees and redemption penalties. Many lenders entice borrowers with a very low headline interest rate and then catch them out with lots of additional fees and penalties. For this reason, the 'best buy' comparison tables for mortgages are often, unintentionally, misleading because they do a great job of ranking mortgage products by interest rate alone. An independent mortgage consultant can review the whole of the market on your behalf and will consider much more than just the interest rate on offer.

> What is important is the *total* cost of the mortgage over a given time period.

Early mortgage repayment rocks!

Repaying your mortgage is one of the most effective ways to retire 10 years early. Here's why.

Your monthly mortgage payments work in one of two ways. You either pay just the interest or you pay back the capital as well as the interest. Let's assume that you do the latter as even people

> Repaying your mortgage is one of the most effective ways to retire 10 years early.

who only pay the interest have to find a way to repay the capital as well at some point in the future.

With a capital repayment mortgage – the formal name for a mortgage where you pay the interest and the capital each month – the shape of the repayments is a little odd. In the early years of the mortgage, most of your monthly payments go towards the interest charges. Only a very small proportion of what you pay each month actually pays off the debt. The amount will vary depending on the term of your mortgage, the interest rate and how big the loan is. It is safe to say that a substantial amount each month goes towards interest rather than capital.

As time goes by, the money you owe on your mortgage gradually reduces. Because there is less capital to repay, the interest charge reduces. The total you pay back each month stays roughly the same and only varies in line with changes in interest rates.

Sometime during the life of your mortgage, the balance shifts. Gradually you start to pay off more and more capital each month and less of your money goes towards interest charges. When the balance shifts, the repayment of your mortgage accelerates.

Here are some examples.

Assume that you have a mortgage of £100,000 (a bit on the small side, given today's property market, but this is nice and easy to base your own calculations on) and an interest rate of 5.75 per cent over a 25-year term. Then, your monthly repayment would be £629. Over the life of the mortgage, you would pay back a total of £188,732. That's almost £90,000 worth of interest charges!

Let's imagine you overpaid by £50, increasing your monthly payments to £679. Your total payments would equal £173,713 and the mortgage term would be reduced by almost 4 years.

Paying back just £50 per month extra would save you £15,019 and bring you 4 years closer to retirement.

Overpaying £100 per month would have an even more significant impact. Your new monthly payment would be £729, but the total repaid over the life of the mortgage would drop to £163,294 – a saving of £25,438. More importantly, your mortgage would be fully repaid in just 18.7 years rather than the traditional 25 years.

Now, let's imagine that you could find an additional £250 each month to overpay your mortgage. The new monthly payment would be £879, but you would save a total of £43,890 in interest charges (paying back a total of £144,842 on your £100,000 borrowed) and reduce your mortgage term by 11.3 years to 13.7 years.

So, on this £100,000 mortgage, you would need to overpay by around £250 per month to pay off your mortgage more than 10 years earlier. Assuming that your mortgage is your single largest item of expenditure each month, then this course of action could, in combination with the other suggestions in this book, enable you to retire 10 years early.

If you want to play around with some numbers based on your own personal circumstances, then just run an Internet search for the term 'mortgage overpayments calculator'. There are plenty of these available online that will let you input the mortgage amount, interest rate, term and the level of overpayment you wish to make. They will then crunch the numbers for you and show how much you could save and how quickly your mortgage would be fully repaid.

Some words of warning

While making regular mortgage overpayments is a very effective use of your money, there are some important words of warning as well.

1 **Watch out for penalties.** Many mortgage products come with redemption penalties – that is, financial charges that are imposed if you pay back more than you originally agreed. Increasingly, mortgage lenders are designing products that will allow you to overpay a certain percentage of your mortgage each month, but there are still plenty around that will penalise you for trying to speed up the repayment of your mortgage.

2 **Don't stretch yourself too far.** Once people understand the power of mortgage overpayments, they can get very excited at the prospect. The temptation exists to start scraping together every available penny and using all of your wealth to pay back the mortgage. This can leave you in a difficult position if an unexpected item of expenditure crops up later in the month. Always leave some space in your budget for things that you do not anticipate spending your money on. A tight budget is one doomed to failure.

3 **Remember that overpayments are effectively being locked away in the value of your home.** If you overpay on your mortgage, then the only ways to get access to that money again are to either sell your home or remortgage to borrow against the property. For this very important reason, many people who like the idea of overpaying their mortgage are turning to a more modern mortgage concept – offset.

The power of offset

When you pay your mortgage each month, you do so out of income that has been taxed. The more you earn, the more you get taxed. A high earner, paying income tax at the rate of 40 per cent, needs to earn £167 for every £100 of mortgage repayment. If you pay the basic rate of income tax, you need to earn £128 for every £100 of mortgage repayment.

When you invest money, the returns are taxed. The simplest example here is the interest you get on savings. If your savings generate £100 of interest, then you get to keep either £80 or £60, depending on whether you are a basic or a higher rate income tax payer.

Tax on earnings and tax on savings or investments mean a double whammy for those trying to repay their mortgage and invest their money at the same time.

Using the £100,000 mortgage example again, with an interest rate of 5.75 per cent, the basic rate tax payer would need to receive pre-tax savings interest of 7.37 per cent each year to keep pace with the interest on the mortgage. The higher rate tax payer would need returns of 9.58 per cent each year to do so.

It is impossible to net these levels of return from the interest on cash savings. It might be possible to get them from investments in property or the stock markets but, then

■ you would also need to pay investment charges, which could increase the return needed by as much as 2 per cent each year

■ your money would be at greater risk over the short term.

For people with savings as well as mortgage debt, there is an alternative to using the cash to repay part of your mortgage.

An offset or current account mortgage is a modern mortgage product that allows you to 'link' the money you have in savings to the debt you have on your mortgage. Any interest that would normally be paid on your savings, and subjected to income tax, is offset against the interest due on the equivalent part of your mortgage. This makes an offset account very tax efficient and gives you continued access to your savings.

In fact, for many people, an offset mortgage will represent a very attractive tax-free investment return with minimal levels of investment risk. Where else could a higher rate tax payer get tax-free investment returns equivalent to 7.37 per cent each year without much risk?

> For many people, an offset mortgage will represent a very attractive tax-free investment return with minimal levels of investment risk.

Here are a couple of examples to demonstrate the power of offset.

Imagine that you have a £100,000 mortgage and £10,000 in your savings account. You are charged interest on the mortgage at 5.75 per cent, so you pay £479 in interest charges each month (£5748 a year).

You receive 5.75 per cent gross interest on your £10,000 in savings. Depending on your income tax status, you either receive £456 or £348 interest net each year. The end result is a cost of £5292 for a basic rate tax payer or £5400 for a higher rate tax payer.

Alternatively, you could offset the £10,000 you have in savings against the mortgage. Then, you would not get any interest on your savings, but only pay interest on £90,000 of your mortgage (the £100,000 mortgage less £10,000 savings). The interest charge would reduce to £5175 a year, saving you £117 each year as a basic rate tax payer or £225 each year as a higher rate tax payer.

These are not particularly big numbers, but, for higher rate tax payers with big mortgages and more available to offset in savings, the tax benefits of an offset mortgage start to really add up.

The most modern offset mortgage accounts allow you to link more than just a savings account to your mortgage. You can link your current account, credit cards and personal loans so the interest you pay each month is calculated based on the difference between all of your liquid assets and all of your debt. This approach means that you receive a much higher rate of interest on your savings and are charged a much lower rate of interest on your unsecured debts.

Some things to watch out for

As with all things financial, there are various potential drawbacks to watch out for with offset or current account mortgages.

1 **Not all offset mortgages are born equal.** The terms and conditions applied to offset mortgages vary wildly from one lender to another. Some offer minimal flexibility, so you need to spend time reading the small print to ensure that your selected mortgage product fits your plans.

2 **The rates can vary.** Most offset and current account mortgages are based on variable interest rates. This means that you cannot fix the interest rate for a period of time and gain the certainty of knowing what your total mortgage cost is going to be each month. The benefit of the variable rate approach, however, is a lot greater flexibility when it comes to repaying or overpaying your mortgage. Very few penalties exist with offset mortgages, but you should still read the small print.

3 **The additional flexibility comes at a price.** Offset mortgages can be a lot more expensive than their traditional mortgage alternatives. This additional price is normally reflected in a higher interest rate and additional set-up fees. More recently, the cost of offset mortgages does appear to have fallen and they should continue to become cheaper as they become a more widespread mortgage solution and as better technology supports the products.

4 **A simpler alternative exists.** If you only have a small amount in savings to offset, then using a cash Individual Savings

Account (ISA) is a good alternative to consider. You can use an ISA to get tax-free interest on your savings and they usually offer a very attractive interest rate that is in line with the interest rates on the most competitive mortgages. The drawback is that you are limited to saving £3000 each year (£3200 from 6 April 2008) into these products, but, for people with smaller amounts of savings, they offer a good alternative to a more complicated offset mortgage.

Financial vehicles for a smooth ride to early retirement

" It's been quite a ride. I loved every minute of it.

Charlton Heston (1924–)

05

There is a range of financial tools that you can use to enable an early retirement. These often look and feel complicated, but, once you understand how they work, you will quickly realise how very simple they can be.

It is difficult to talk about early retirement planning without talking about pensions. These financial instruments are clearly linked to retirement planning and, for most people, form the main part of their retirement plans. Pension planning and retirement planning are two very different things, however. Pensions do play a valuable role within early retirement planning, but the non-pension alternatives are as important to understand and consider.

In this chapter, we are going to look at the whole range of financial vehicles that you can use to enable an early retirement. We will also talk about the advantages and disadvantages of using a traditional pension plan. Pensions may be important, but they are not the only solution if you are planning for an early retirement. This chapter finishes by looking at the non-pension alternatives.

Financial tools and vehicles

The range of different financial and investment options available today is bewildering. There are more investment funds in the UK than actual companies on the stock market that you can invest in. Keeping up to speed with the changes to products and investments is a full-time job that requires the use of sophisticated computer systems. Even then it is possible that a new product will slip by unnoticed.

Yet, financial products can be a big help when you are following your RTYE plan. They can be used to speed up your progress towards your ultimate goal of an early retirement. The right

Financial products can be a big help when you are following your RTYE plan.

investment in the right product can be a massive helping hand towards achieving your goals.

The wrong investment or the wrong financial product, on the other hand, can be a big hindrance. It can slow down your progress. Many people who have experienced the wrong product will be put off retirement planning for life. They will treat all investments in the future with a degree of suspicion.

To succeed with your RTYE plan, you need to treat investments with a healthy dose of scepticism. For the most part, the investments and financial products available today are reasonably good. There is far more transparency now than there was during the 1980s and early 1990s. Products being promoted by insurance companies and other financial institutions are now competitively priced and easy to understand.

A few 'dogs' remain and there are important things to be aware of. If you know which features to watch out for, then your experience with investments for retirement planning is likely to be a good one.

The difference between products and investments

Before we go much further, it is important to understand the difference between products and investments.

■ Products are the wrappers that give you access to investments. For example, personal pensions and Individual Savings Accounts (ISAs) are both types of products. They are not an investment on their own, but something that wraps around the investments you select.

■ Investments are the underlying things that you put your money in. These sit within the products and often take the form of funds, which are a way of investing in different things.

It is important to know the difference between products and investments. Too many people claim that 'pensions are bad' because they don't understand that the pension is just the wrapper. The investments they selected within the pension plan might well be 'bad', but the pension itself is rarely the problem.

Five things to watch out for

Whenever we select a financial product for a client there are at least five factors that we consider, in detail. These are factors that are key to ensuring that a suitable product is selected – one that will 'do what it says on the tin' and meet expectations.

Some factors are more important than others, so, depending on your circumstances and objectives, you may wish to put a greater degree of emphasis on some items in this list than on the rest.

1 **Open and transparent charges.** Far too many financial products still have convoluted charging structures that appear to have been designed to confuse and bamboozle the end user. The secret here is to keep things simple. Any product that takes the smoke and mirrors approach to product charging is best avoided. Look for products that have explicit charges so you can see exactly what you are paying for. There is no such thing as a free lunch, but transparency is essential. You should be able to see exactly how much the provision of the financial product and the fund management is, as well as if there are any charges for advice.

2 **Service standards.** Your experience of a particular financial product will often come down to the experience you have

with the provider that manages it. Insurance companies have a rightly deserved reputation for poor service. It can often take weeks to complete the simplest instruction, assuming they follow the instruction correctly in the first place. Finding a product provider with high standards of service is a challenge, but well worth the effort it takes. Your satisfaction with a particular provider will depend on how good it is at servicing the product you have purchased.

3 **Range of funds.** The financial product is just a wrapper. The really important factor, most of the time, is the range of investment funds you can access within the product. The old days of a product offering funds from a single company are long gone. Always demand a product with which you can access investment funds from a wide range of leading fund managers. You might have to pay a bit extra to access these 'external' funds, but it can often be a price worth paying. If performance from these external funds exceeds that available from the funds on offer from the product provider, then paying a few extra pounds a year for the privilege is a good use of your money.

4 **Financial strength.** Retirement planning is a long-term thing. Knowing that the company you select will still be around in a few years' time will prevent many sleepless nights and trauma in the future. Sticking to product providers that demonstrate a high level of financial strength is a good way of avoiding those sleepless nights. After working hard towards an early retirement for most of your working life, the last thing you want to experience is the company managing your pension going bust. To assess financial strength, look for independent ratings from credit analysts such as Standard & Poors. Anything less than a financially strong company will probably not make the shortlist for your RTYE plans.

5 **Flexibility.** This is a fairly general term that covers a number of important features. It is important to look for a product

that gives you as much flexibility as possible. It is particularly important that this flexibility comes without additional cost. Make sure that the products you choose allow you to take your money out earlier than planned and make other changes throughout the time they are in operation. These might include changes to investment funds or the amounts you invest. Your circumstances and objectives will change over time so it is important that the financial products you use can reflect these changes.

The 'p' word

A few years ago I was a guest on a radio show and we were taking questions about retirement planning from callers. Just before the 'on air' light turned red, the presenter turned to me and said 'just try to avoid using the word "pension"'. Now, talking live on radio for an hour about retirement planning without using the 'p' word was a challenge, to say the least, and within the first five minutes I had failed.

Pensions often get a bad press. You only need to pick up any Sunday newspaper and turn to the money section to find pension-related horror stories. If we all believed everything we read in the papers, it would be a wonder if anyone still used pensions.

Of course, people still do use pensions. When they reach retirement, the vast majority of pension owners are pleased that they did start a pension. The alternative – living on meagre State pension benefits – is not an attractive option.

The basics

To understand pensions, you need to know the basics. At their simplest, pension plans are financial products specifically

> **Pension plans are financial products designed to help you invest for your retirement.**

designed to help you invest for your retirement. They provide a home for you to invest your money for the long term.

There are three stages in a typical pension plan – putting money in, investing money in the pension plan and taking money out. Let's take a closer look at each of these.

Putting money in

When you put money into a pension, it is called a 'contribution'. This money can come from you, your employer or even the State in the form of National Insurance contribution rebates.

We could all put up to 100 per cent of our salaries into pensions each tax year if we wanted to. Since 2001, this option is even available to babies and children. If you don't have any earnings to justify a pension contribution, you can still invest money and get tax relief on these contributions. The annual contribution limit for people with no earnings, including babies and children, is £3600.

The main motivation for putting money into a pension fund to save for your retirement is the tax relief you receive for doing so. For every £1 you put into a pension, the taxman will automatically add a further 28p to your pension fund. If you pay higher rate income tax, you can even claim a bit more tax relief. You can find more on this and how it works, in detail, in Chapter 8.

Investing money

Once your contributions are inside the pension wrapper, you can decide how to invest this money. Traditional pension plans give you access to a reasonably good range of investment funds. This means that a professional fund manager takes your money, adds it to money from other investors and invests it in line with the objectives of the fund.

This approach to investing saves a great deal of time and money. It is also an effective way to reduce risk because your money is spread over a larger number of investments than it would be if you invested it directly on your own.

Taking money out

When it comes to taking money out of a pension, the rules can be very complicated. At their simplest, up to one quarter of your pension fund can be taken as cash and the rest of the fund has to provide your retirement income.

There are a number of different ways in which it can provide this income, but the one that most people choose is to buy a financial instrument called an 'annuity'. The way this works is that you hand over your pension fund to an insurance company and it guarantees to pay you an income for life.

You cannot take money out of a pension until you are 50 years old. This minimum age is going up to 55 years old from 6 April 2010.

The problems with pensions

Pensions make a great retirement planning tool. The tax relief you receive while you are making contributions is a powerful incentive to lock your money away in a pension fund for the long term. For most people, a pension fund is a sensible choice of retirement planning vehicle.

You are not 'most people', though. As a reader of this book, you want more from your financial life. A pension plan may or may not be the most suitable way to achieve your plans for an early retirement.

> **You are not 'most people', you want more from your financial life.**

There are a few potential problems with pensions that could get in the way of your RTYE plan:

1 **Lack of flexibility when it comes to taking benefits.** The minimum retirement age of 50 or 55 means that it is impossible to get hold of the cash in your pension once you have made a contribution. The money is locked away for a very long time. This prevents you from gaining access to the money any earlier than the minimum retirement age, which may not coincide with your plans for an early retirement.

2 **Perceived poor annuity rates when you retire.** Buying an annuity is a very good way to secure an income for life. The problem with this is that annuity rates are based on, among other things, how long you are likely to live. This means that you only get better rates when you are older. If you buy an annuity at 50 or 55 years old, the annuity rate is going to be very low. Once you secure the annuity at that low rate, it is fixed for life. This means that using a pension to plan for an early retirement and then buying an annuity is probably not a very effective use of your money.

3 **It's difficult to get excited about pensions.** Try as hard as you might, it's tough to get excited about pensions. People associate the word 'pension' with old age, expensive charges and complicated rules. It's not the sort of thing that makes good dinner party conversation. Part of the problem with pensions is they are not very tangible – it is difficult to touch and feel your pension plan.

A possible solution

If these really are the three biggest problems associated with pensions, then there just might be a solution.

A Self-Invested Personal Pension (SIPP) is a special type of personal pension. It is run according to the same rules as a traditional personal pension, but offers investors much more control and flexibility in three main areas.

1 A SIPP allows you to put money into a far greater range of investments than a traditional pension. While a conventional personal pension plan limits you to investing your money in the company's own or externally managed investment funds, a SIPP opens up almost the entire investment universe. Thus, via a SIPP, it is possible to access a very wide range of investments. These include listed or unlisted companies and commercial property. You are not restricted to a single investment company or even a small panel of investment funds from different investment companies. A SIPP opens up a world of investment possibility.

2 The charges are much more transparent with a SIPP. Admittedly the charges associated with personal pension plans have been getting much clearer over recent years. The vast majority now have a single charge, shown as a percentage of the value of your pension fund each year – known as the annual management charge. This annual management charge pays for your investments, the administration of the pension plan and provides remuneration for the adviser. Even so, with a SIPP, the charges are listed separately so you can easily see the costs associated with investment, administration and advice. This makes it much easier to determine whether or not these charges represent good value for money.

3 The final area in which a SIPP offers more control and flexibility is when it comes to taking retirement benefits. You can leave a SIPP invested when you choose to retire and draw an

income directly from the pension fund, rather than exchange your money for an annuity. This retirement option is known as an unsecured pension, but used to be called income drawdown. It comes with some fairly healthy risks, but, for investors who want additional flexibility and control, particularly when retiring early, it is a valuable retirement option.

It's not all good news

As with everything in the world of financial planning, where there are positive features, there must also be some drawbacks. SIPPs are no exception to this rule.

> Where there are positive features, there must also be some drawbacks. SIPPs are no exception.

The biggest disadvantages of using a SIPP instead of a personal pension are costs, complexity and restrictions.

SIPPs tend to cost more than conventional personal pensions. The additional control and flexibility you gain from using a SIPP tends to come at a higher price. This is not unusual for a 'premium' product like a SIPP, so the big question you need to ask is, 'What additional value do I get?' If a SIPP enables you to take greater control over your retirement planning and fully understand what your pension contains, then this extra cost might be a small price to pay for the added peace of mind.

There is also additional complexity to contend with when you use a SIPP for retirement planning. This complexity comes about as a result of the greater investment choice and choices open to you when you reach retirement. Working alongside a professional adviser will help to reduce this complexity, but you should be prepared to do some additional reading before you start using a SIPP.

The restrictions when using a SIPP mainly surround the investment of 'protected rights' funds within this type of pension. 'Protected rights' is the name given to the part of a pension fund made up from National Insurance rebates when you opt out of the State Second Pension. As things stand, you are not allowed to self-invest 'protected rights' via a SIPP. There is some speculation that this rule will change in the very near future. Until that time, though, you will need to keep your protected rights pension fund in a separate, non-SIPP pension plan.

Turning your pension fund into income

When you decide to take benefits from your pension fund, you have to make a number of tough choices. Possibly the toughest choice is how you convert the pension fund into an income. There are several different ways to do this. We have already touched on some of these, but let us look at the three main choices and what they mean, plus a further option.

Annuity purchase

The commonest way to turn your pension fund into income is to buy an annuity. This is a financial instrument offered by insurance companies and it is a simple way to create a guaranteed stream of income for the rest of your life. People like annuities because they offer a high level of certainty. Once you have made the decision to buy an annuity with your pension fund, there is very little in the way of ongoing management. Each and every month an income payment will arrive in your bank account. This will continue for as long as you live and possibly for longer if you have paid extra for additional features.

> It can represent a very poor return. This is
> particularly relevant when you want to retire 10
> years early.

Annuities are not loved by everybody, however. Because the
annuity rate you will get depends on numerous factors
(including life expectancy, interest rates and the structure of the
annuity you choose), it can represent a very poor return on your
investment. This is particularly relevant when you want to retire
10 years early.

The following examples are based on the most competitive
annuity rates I was able to find when I wrote this book. The
rates fluctuate on a regular basis and there is a huge difference
between the most and least competitive providers. Always shop
around when you are thinking of buying an annuity with your
pension fund to make sure that you get the best deal.

The following examples assume that you buy an annuity for
£100,000. I have picked this number not because it is an
average pension fund size, but because it makes it much
easier to do your own calculations. The figures that follow
also assume the income from the annuity remains level for
the rest of your life (no inflation proofing) and that the payments are guaranteed for a minimum of five years. There are
literally hundreds of different variations available when
researching an annuity rate, which is why professional and
independent advice should always be sought if you are
thinking of buying one.

Annuity rates are significantly worse if you buy them early. As
an example, a man aged 65 could secure an income of £7480 a
year. The same man would only get £6740 a year at the age of
60 or £6240 at 55. This represents nearly 10 per cent less

income if you retire 5 years early and almost 17 per cent less if you retire 10 years early.

For a woman, the drop in income for taking benefits early is just as stark. The best annuity for a woman aged 60 would pay £6440 a year. If she took an annuity at 55 years old, it would pay £6120 a year and only £5880 a year at 50 years old. That means almost 5 per cent less income for retiring 5 years early and 9 per cent less for retiring 10 years early.

When you bear in mind that this means a lower income for every year you receive the annuity income, these are substantial reductions.

Life expectancy is a big driver of annuity rates. You can get a better annuity rate if you are a smoker because the insurance company assumes that you will die sooner and it will have to pay the income for a shorter period of time. Most annuity providers define a smoker as somebody who has smoked at least 10 cigarettes a day for the last 10 years. They can and will ask you to provide a saliva sample to prove that you are a smoker, so don't lie on the application form just to get a better annuity rate!

A male smoker aged 55 years old could get an annuity income of £7080 a year compared to £6240 a year for his non-smoking counterpart. That is £840 a year more or 13.5 per cent – quite a big increase, due to the shorter life expectancy of a smoker.

For a 50-year-old female smoker, the best annuity rate for this size of pension fund is £6430 a year compared to £5880 a year for a non-smoker. That is an increase of £550 a year or just over 9 per cent.

Investment-linked annuity

The alternative to a conventional annuity paying you a guaranteed income is an investment-linked annuity. This particular financial product is not particularly popular in the UK due to limited availability and some other fairly unattractive features.

This option offers you a higher rate of income in the future than you would receive from a conventional annuity, but comes with added risk. Because your income is linked to different investments, including company shares, it can go up or down each year. You can pick investment funds to suit your own attitude towards investment risk, but it still represents a higher level of risk than a conventional annuity. If you need a certain level of income each year, then this sort of annuity is probably not suitable for you.

You can choose to convert an investment-linked annuity to a conventional annuity, but you are often tied in to the rates on offer from one annuity provider. This may not offer you the best value, so be very careful when picking an investment-linked annuity provider to make sure that it is also a competitive conventional annuity provider.

Unsecured pension

This is a more radical option than buying an annuity with your pension fund, but it is becoming much more popular than in the past. It involves you leaving your pension fund invested and then taking an income directly from the pension fund. You can choose how much income you want to take each year, from zero up to a maximum level, which is recalculated every five years.

It is possible to use unsecured income to provide an income in retirement until you reach 75 years old. At that age, you have to either buy a conventional annuity with what is left in your pension fund or move into something called an alternatively secured pension, which comes with some nasty tax penalties.

The main benefit of using the unsecured pension fund is that your pension is still invested, so it has the chance to grow in the future. When you buy a conventional annuity with your pension fund, you are converting the value of the fund at a certain date into an income for life. An unsecured pension prevents you from having to do this. This retirement option also offers a lot more flexibility over things such as income levels and the timing of this income.

As your money stays invested, there are also some risks associated with an unsecured pension. One of the attractions of using a conventional annuity is that you benefit from the earlier than expected death of other annuity holders. I know that sounds morbid, but it is an actuarially accepted way of working out the rate you get on an annuity. The longer you defer buying an annuity, the more of it you miss out on.

The other big drawback is charges. With a conventional annuity, the charges are all included within the annuity rate you receive. With an unsecured pension, however, the charges are clearly visible and higher as a result of the ongoing management required. You will probably need to pay for ongoing advice from a professional who can help you manage the investments in your unsecured pension plan.

All or some of the above

Keep in mind that you do not need to use your entire pension fund with each of these options. It is possible, and often encouraged, to divide your pension fund into segments and then 'phase' the taking of benefits over time.

The main advantage of this approach is that you can take a small part of your tax-free cash entitlement each time you take benefits from one or more segments. This tax-free cash effectively reduces the amount of income tax you would normally pay on annuity or unsecured pension income. This approach works particularly well if you need income during retirement rather than a one-off capital sum when you first decide to retire.

The other advantage of this phased approach to buying retirement benefits is that you will be able to buy annuity income at different times as you get older. This should mean that you get a better annuity rate each year as you will be a year older and have a slightly shorter life expectancy. There is no guarantee that your annuity income will improve year on year, but the odds should be stacked in your favour.

Whatever you do ...

... get professional advice! Making decisions about what to do with your hard-earned pension fund, which you may have built up over 30 years or more, requires expert advice and serious consideration. The choices and options are numerous and, once decisions have been made, they cannot always be reversed at a later date.

With early retirement, you are likely to live much longer during retirement so the choices you make about your pension fund will have to sustain your lifestyle for many years to come. In a lot of cases, your pension fund will have to last for almost as long as you spent building it up. Get expert advice and make your decisions with care.

> Get expert advice and make your decisions with care.

The non-pension alternatives

The best retirement plans that I have seen consist of more than just a well-managed pension fund. The top retirement planners combine a whole variety of pension and non-pension assets to give themselves a greater degree of flexibility and control over their plans for retirement.

There are a number of non-pension alternatives you should consider when planning for your early retirement.

> **The best retirement plans consist of more than just a well-managed pension fund.**

Tax-free investments

Individual Savings Accounts (ISAs) are a popular investment choice for early retirement planning. Just like pensions, they are an investment wrapper rather than an investment in their own right. Also just like pensions, they offer some generous tax benefits to investors.

Payments made into an ISA do not benefit from any tax relief. The £1 you put in is a £1 that is invested. To make up for this lack of up front tax relief on investments, there are some tax advantages to having an ISA and when you take the money out at the other end.

Money invested in an ISA is largely free of tax. This means you are not taxed if the investment grows in value and you are not taxed on any income generated within the ISA. There is one small exception to this rule and it is a minor technical point about the way companies can reclaim tax paid on their profits. The bulk of investment returns within an ISA remain tax-free.

When you come to take money out of an ISA, there is no tax to pay at that point either. All in all, this makes for a fairly generous set of tax advantages when you invest your money in an

ISA. Because of these tax advantages, there is a limit on how much you can pay into an ISA each tax year. These investment restrictions prevent investors from piling too much money into an ISA and then not paying any tax on the returns.

For a Maxi ISA (the kind that enables you to invest in a wide range of funds) this investment limit is set at £7000 each tax year or £7200 from 6 April 2008. For a Mini ISA, investing in cash, the annual limit is £3000 or £3600 from 6 April 2008. You can pay up to £4000 each tax year into a Mini ISA, investing in a wide range of different funds. You cannot invest in a Maxi *and* a Mini ISA during the same tax year.

On the same date that the limit is to be raised, the distinction between a Maxi and Mini ISA will also be removed. This should make ISAs much easier to understand and more popular for early retirement planning.

One reason ISAs are so well suited to planning for early retirement is the lack of restrictions when it comes to taking the money out. There are no minimum ages and no rules about how much you can take as cash or income. It is your money and you can access it at any time. This makes an ISA a good partner for a pension plan, supplementing it when you retire early. Your pension gives you a benefit in a predetermined format when you reach a certain age. Your ISA is available to fill any gaps.

Other investments

Once you have utilised your tax-efficient investment limits, you might consider using other investment options to help build up wealth for an early retirement. In Chapter 8, we will look at how these non-tax-efficient investments can be structured to reduce your tax liability and maximise returns. Just because you invest outside of an ISA wrapper does not automatically mean that you need to pay tax on the returns.

When investing outside of an ISA, you can choose to put your money into collective investments (such as unit trusts, open-ended investment companies or investment trusts) or direct investments.

Collective investments mean that you pool your money with other investors and delegate the day-to-day management of the investment to a professional investment manager. Doing this has a number of benefits. One of these is that it reduces the cost of investing. As one of many investors, you benefit from economies of scale. These cost savings are partially outweighed by the cost of the fund manager who takes responsibility for investing your money. Collective investments are the ideal solution for those who have relatively modest amounts to invest, little investment expertise or not enough time to proactively manage their investments.

Direct investment in company shares or other investment instruments gives you a lot more control over how your money is invested on a day-to-day basis. Investing directly in company shares is not for the faint-hearted, however, as it is difficult to spread the risk unless you have a large amount of money to invest. Also, even with the reduced dealing costs associated with Internet stockbrokers, it is still relatively expensive to buy and sell company shares. Thus, this option is best reserved for wealthier investors, those with particular investment expertise and people with plenty of time available to research, monitor and trade their investments.

Investing in property

The rise in property prices and the low interest rates of the past five years has made property investment a more viable alternative to pensions for retirement planning. Buying a residential property with the intention of letting it to a tenant (buy to let) can provide a good way to build up wealth for your early retirement.

Buy to let investing is effective for a number of reasons.

1 You can borrow money to make the investment. A typical buy to let mortgage only requires that you put down a 15 per cent deposit. Some mortgage lenders ask for an even smaller deposit than this. Borrowing money to invest means that you are effectively using somebody else's money to make your investment. You pay them for the privilege in the form of interest, but it gives you access to a bigger investment than you would otherwise be able to afford.

2 The rental income should cover the cost of this borrowing. The rent paid by the tenant who lives in the property should be enough to pay the mortgage and other costs each month. Many buy to let mortgage lenders insist that the rent is at least 120 per cent of the mortgage interest. This means that a £200,000 property with a £170,000 buy to let mortgage and an interest rate of 5.5 per cent would need to bring in rental income of at least £935 a month to make it a viable option.

3 As well as the rental income, you should benefit from long-term capital growth. As an asset class, residential property can go down as well as up in value. Over the longer term (say, 10 to 20 years), you could have a reasonable expectation that it would grow in value at a faster rate than price inflation. If the tenants have been paying your mortgage costs over this period, then you can be left with a sizeable investment return when you come to retire.

As with all retirement plans, it does not make sense to keep all your eggs in one basket. There are numerous risks associated with buy to let investing. These include interest rates going up, property prices falling and difficulty in finding a tenant who wants to live in your property and pay rent. You may also be faced with costly property repairs and maintenance.

If you don't fancy the idea of becoming a landlord, but you do want to consider this as an investment option, it is possible to pay for the services of a property management company. If you do this, then be prepared to pay around two months' worth of rental income each year for the privilege. You might consider that expensive, but it might be a small price to pay for avoiding a 4 a.m. phone call telling you that a pipe has burst!

Cash

Investment experts say that cash is king. Money in your bank or building society account should form the cornerstone of your financial plans for retirement. It does not make sense to keep too much of your wealth in cash, though, because price inflation can erode its real value. However, there are some major advantages to keeping some of your retirement funds in cash form.

1 **You can get your hands on it in an emergency.** Cash is the most liquid form of investment. To get hold of money in other investments can take time and result in you having to accept a lower price than you want to when you sell them. For example, consider the likely consequences of needing to sell your house very quickly. You should always aim to have an 'emergency fund' of around three to six months' typical expenditure in cash that you can easily lay your hands on.

2 **It is good for diversification.** Intelligent investing is all about spreading your money across more than one asset class. If you invest in things such as company shares and property, it is sensible to keep some of your wealth in cash in case these asset classes fall in value.

3 **You can take advantage of opportunities.** Keeping some money in cash means that you can take advantage of investment opportunities as and when they arise. If you spot what you consider to be a cheap investment, then having some cash available can make the difference between buying that investment and missing out on an opportunity.

Taking risks

“Take calculated risks. That is quite different from
being rash.

George S. Patton (1885–1945)

06

> **Investment risk can actively help you with your early retirement planning.**

With greater risk comes the chance of a greater financial reward. That is why investment risk can actively help you with your early retirement planning. By understanding how much risk you can take with your money, it is possible to create an effective investment strategy for early retirement.

In this chapter we will discuss risk and the role it plans in your RTYE plan. Taking more risk can lead to higher investment returns, which will speed up your progress with the RTYE plan. It can also lead to bigger losses, which will act as a set back.

It is very important to know how much risk you can afford to take and when you can afford to take it. This chapter also looks at when it is the right time to take more investment risk with your plans for retirement.

We finish by looking at a powerful way to control the amount of risk you take by means of what is known as asset allocation. This is an investment process we use with our clients to ensure that they only take a level of risk with their money they feel comfortable with. It is based on a complicated scientific theory, but the practical application of this investment process is very straightforward.

The relationship between risk and reward

Before we move on, it is important to understand the relationship between risk and reward. This can be summed up by saying that more risk equals more reward and less risk equals less reward.

> **More risk equals the _potential_ for more reward. There is no guarantee.**

In truth, we should say that more risk equals the _potential_ for more reward. There is no guarantee that, by taking more risk with your money, you will automatically reap the rewards and see your wealth go sky high.

Risk and reward have an unbreakable relationship. This means that it is not possible to have more of one without more of the other. Many people will try to convince you that you can get massive investment returns with no risk. Unfortunately, it is not possible. Indeed, anybody who tries to tell you otherwise should be treated with extreme caution. Such a person either doesn't understand the relationship between risk and reward or does understand it and is trying to sell you an investment that is far riskier than he or she is prepared to say. Either way, you should start walking away from that person, very quickly!

Risk and retirement planning

The traditional view is that risk is more acceptable with retirement planning than in other areas of your personal financial planning. People are more likely to accept a bit of risk with their pension funds than they are, for example, with the repayment of their mortgage. There are several reasons for this.

1 Time. Because, typically, retirement is a long way in the future (at least it is when we start planning for it), people are prepared to take more risk. If their investments fall in value, there is plenty of time for them to recover. A stock market crash when there is 20 years to go before you retire is no cause for concern. There is plenty of time for your pension fund value to go back up again. In fact, over that sort of time period, you might expect a whole series of stock market falls before they recover again. It is the long-term performance of your investments that you are bothered about, not the short-term bumps along the way.

2 **Ownership.** Because pension funds are not readily accessible sources of cash, we tend to be less worried about them. They are not something we can touch or feel. They are often created not with our own money but with contributions from our employer. This lack of direct ownership causes people to be less concerned about how the pension fund is invested and how much risk is being taken. A pension is, after all, just numbers on a piece of paper each year – that is, until you actually come to take benefits from the plan.

3 **Understanding.** This is still a major reason for people not taking an active interest in the way their plans for retirement are actually invested. Because we don't always understand how a pension plan works, we take less of an interest in the way it is invested. Many investors I work with who have existing pension plans are shocked to discover the level of risk being taken with them. In the majority of cases, their plans are taking too little or too much risk for their liking. Before speaking to me, they had no idea and just expected their pension funds to be suitably invested. The reality is often very different.

Are these good reasons?

With the exception of the first reason, the other two are fairly lousy reasons for taking more risk with your retirement plans. That is not to say it is wrong to take more risk with your plans for retirement, but it *is* wrong to take more risk without having a good reason for doing so.

Time is an excellent reason for taking more risk with your investments than you would do under other circumstances. Even with the intention to retire 10 years early, there is a good chance that your money will be invested for a long period of time.

The general rule of thumb here is that you can take a greater degree of investment risk when the timescale is long. With anything less than five years, you should probably stick to very safe investments. For a 5- to 15-year investment period, it makes sense to invest in line with your ordinary attitude towards investment risk. For investments over 15 years long, however, all bets are off. Go for the maximum level of risk you can afford to take without it keeping you awake every night. My team and I are responsible for advising clients how to invest tens of millions of pounds' worth of investments. We all sleep easily at night, not because we don't care (we certainly do!), but because all of the advice we give is based on a thorough understanding of how much risk the client is comfortable taking.

> The general rule of thumb is that you can take a greater degree of investment risk when the timescale is long.

The ownership argument for not controlling investment risk is only partially valid. While you cannot get your hands on any part of your pension fund before the age of 50 (or 55 from 2010), it is your money. Even the part of your pension fund that was created because of employer contributions belongs to you. You own the money, but it is designated for a future purpose – to provide benefits during your retirement. While the money in your pension plan might not be accessible, it is important, so you should invest it in a way that you feel comfortable with.

The understanding argument is valid, but only if you don't want to understand how your plans for retirement work. As a reader of this book, you do want to understand and have taken steps to make sense of your retirement plans. Think of pension plans as being like protective wrappers that surround investments there for your retirement. The contents of a pension are just like any other type of investment. They are surprisingly simple, but, as soon as anyone says the word 'pension' or 'retirement plans', people stop listening and assume they are complicated.

As I write this, the UK stock market has taken a bit of a tumble. Investors who had all of their plans for retirement exposed to this one type of investment have lost almost 4 per cent in a single day and over 11 per cent in the last month. If this sort of short-term loss is enough to give you sleepless nights, then you should seriously consider taking less risk with your money. If, on the other hand, you see investment falls like this as being par for the course for the long-term investor, then a higher-risk strategy sounds perfect for you.

Risk and early retirement

Your view of risk may well be different when you consider it in relation to early retirement. It may be different but not necessarily higher or lower.

If you retire 10 years early, then your investments have less time to recover if the markets fall in value. Conventional wisdom is that a shorter investment term requires a more cautious approach. You should take less risk because your objective (early retirement) is sooner.

Conventional wisdom is not what this book is about, however. You want to defy conventional wisdom by retiring 10 years early. Conventional wisdom is for conventional people, not people who want to take control of their retirement plans.

An early retirement means two other important things when it comes to investment risk.

1 **Less time for your money to grow.** This means that you need to take more risk to maximise the chances of growth occurring in the time you have. If you have 10 fewer years to put money towards your plans for early retirement, then you can contribute more towards your retirement plans, take more risk in the expectation of getting higher returns or do a bit of both.

2 **Your money has to last for longer.** When you actually retire, the money you have accumulated (in both pension and non-pension assets) has to last for longer than if you retired at the usual age. It has to last at least 10 years longer. With increasing life expectancy, there is already a great deal of pressure on retirement funds, particularly pension plans, to last for a longer period of time during retirement than was the case in the past. Your plans to retire 10 years early will serve to increase this pressure even more.

These two factors mean that you need to disregard the conventional view of investing for retirement. You need to continue to take more risk rather than reduce your risk profile as the timeframe reduces. There are some important exceptions to this.

The time to take less risk

As you get closer to the date when you plan to retire, you might want to reduce the amount of risk you are taking with your money. This is because a fall in the value of your investments in

> Gradually reduce the amount of risk you are taking in the five years before you want to retire.

the year or so before you retire can have a devastating impact on your plans for an early retirement.

What you should really be aiming to do is gradually reduce the amount of risk you are taking in the five years before you want to retire. By doing this on an annual or six-monthly basis, you can gradually reduce the chances of a nasty shock wiping out a large proportion of your retirement funds.

This is more conventional wisdom from the world of retirement planning. It is particularly good advice if you plan to convert your pension fund into an annuity (as described in the previous chapter). It is not such good advice if you plan to keep your pension fund invested for the first part of your retirement or until you reach the age of 75.

In this instance, you may well want to keep your risk profile exactly the same as you get closer to your chosen early retirement date. There is a chance that your pension fund will drop in value in the days before you retire, but, as you plan to keep the money invested, it will be able to grow again during your retirement and before you finally convert the fund into an annuity income for the rest of your life.

How much risk should you take?

Determining your personal investment risk profile can be difficult as there are so many factors to consider. Before we provide investment advice to our clients, we work through a sophisticated questionnaire that gives us and them some guidance on their risk profile. The rest of the risk-profiling process comes down to a detailed discussion about the level of risk they want to take with their money.

Different investment objectives often have different risk profiles. This is quite common, so your focus now should be on establishing an investment risk profile for your early retirement plans. This may well differ from your plans to save enough to buy a new house next year or repay your mortgage. Your early retirement risk profile is likely to have some links to the risk profile for your other financial objectives.

There are five things that should influence the amount of investment risk you are prepared to take with your retirement plans.

1 **Knowledge.** If you really know your stuff when it comes to investment, then you can afford to take more risk.

2 **Experience.** Knowing what risks you are likely to face because you have faced them before means that you can take more risk with your money.

3 **Reactions.** The way you would react to your investments suddenly dropping value is a good indicator of the level of investment risk you would feel comfortable taking.

4 **Feelings.** How do you normally feel after making a major financial decision? If you feel remorse or guilt, then you should consider adopting a more cautious attitude towards investment risk.

5 **Greed.** If you are greedy when it comes to money and want your investments to grow faster, you need to take more risk. If you would be satisfied with lower returns, then there is no need to take more risk to get higher returns than you want or need.

To accurately establish your attitude towards investment risk, you need to think about these five factors. Don't look at them in isolation – consider all the factors and how they relate to each other. If you are in any doubt about how much risk you feel comfortable with, you should start with a cautious approach. It is always possible to take more risk in the future, but, once you have lost money due to high-risk investments, it is hard to get it back.

The best way to control risk

The single most effective way to control risk in relation to your early retirement plans is to be careful about what you invest in!

Be careful about what you invest in!

There are four main types of investment. Most of the things you invest in fall into one of these four categories. Each different category – or 'asset class' as we prefer to call them – carries with it a different level of investment risk. Here is a brief description of each one and what you can expect from them in terms of risk.

1 **Cash.** This is probably the most familiar asset class and the most cautious form of investment in terms of risk. It's the money you keep in your bank or building society. There is such a low risk for this asset class because the capital value stays the same and the interest added is technically an income. Most people allow this income to accumulate, which makes the cash grow in value. The drawback of this very low level of risk is that the chances of achieving higher returns are extremely limited. While cash is a very predictable asset class, it is not going to make you a millionaire (unless you have a lot of cash to start with!). In some circumstances, the real value of cash can actually go down if the cost of living, measured by price inflation, is higher than the interest rate you get on your money. This makes cash very safe from one perspective but, actually, quite risky from another.

2 **Fixed interest securities.** The second asset class on the risk scale is any investment in debt. This can be debt in either a company or the Government. Company debt is normally called corporate bonds and Government debt is called gilts.

While the rate of interest is agreed at the outset, these investments can go up and down in value. The risk associated with this particular investment asset class can vary a great deal depending on what you invest in. The most cautious fixed-interest securities are typically gilts, which are backed up by the Government. Corporate bonds tend to be riskier, but the level of risk depends on how financially secure is the company that issues the debt.

3 **Property.** The third main investment asset class is property. From an investment perspective, this can mean either residential property (like your house) or commercial property (including shops, offices and warehouses). Property is a riskier investment option again because the value of it can fluctuate, as can the amount of rental income you receive. There is an additional risk when you borrow money to invest in property. If the cost of borrowing – the interest rate – increases faster than your rental income, then you could be left paying the difference between the mortgage payments and the rent you receive.

4 **Equities.** The riskiest main investment asset class is equities – often called company shares. By investing in equities you are participating in the performance of a particular company or group of companies. These investments are often called 'shares' because, as an investor, you 'share' in the good fortune of the business. If they do well, then you can expect the capital value of the equities to go up. They may also be in a better financial position to pay you more income in the form of dividends. As well as how the company performs, other factors can influence the value of the shares when you come to sell them. This includes the way people feel about the future prospects of a particular company, the sector it operates in or even the whole economy.

Where should I invest for my early retirement?

Now that you know what each asset class looks like in terms of investment risk, you need to decide where to invest your money.

Barclays' 'Equity Gilt Study' has been published every year since 1956. It provides a detailed analysis of the annual returns from equities, fixed-interest securities and cash. The study shows that, historically, the best long-term investment returns have come from the riskier asset class – equities. Over a period of 25 years or more, the equities asset class has outperformed all the others.

It is rarely a good idea to invest in a single investment asset class. Even for the lower-risk classes this is a very high-risk approach as it is having all of your financial eggs in one basket. Spreading your investments around across the four main investment asset classes is a much better strategy, regardless of your risk profile.

> Spread your investments around across the four main investment asset classes.

It is, therefore, important to find the right mix of asset classes depending on your risk profile. If you are a very cautious investor, you might decide to put more of your money into the more cautious asset classes – cash and fixed-interest securities. You might still invest some of your money in property and equities, but more of it would be invested in the less risky areas.

> Find the right mix of depending on your risk
> profile.

A more adventurous investor would expose more money to the riskier investment options. You would still consider investing some money in cash and fixed-interest securities, but more of your money would go into property and equities.

Getting this mix, or asset allocation, right is very important because the majority of investment returns come from investing in the correct asset classes. Individual stock or fund selection is far less important than being in the right investment asset class in the first place.

As well as each having a different risk profile, each of the main asset classes also behaves differently from the others. We call this different behaviour 'correlation' and it is important to understand how it works to get the right level of risk with your investments.

'Correlation' is the term used to describe the way that one asset class will behave when another asset class is doing something. For example, if equities are going down in value, there is a good chance that fixed-interest securities will go up in value. This predictable behaviour of the different investment asset classes enables the savvy investor to invest in different asset classes with the expectation that when one is going down in value, at least the others will be going up!

Slash your costs

> A cynic is a man who knows the price of everything but the value of nothing.
> Oscar Wilde (1854–1900)

07

Cutting costs is another effective way to make progress with your plans to retire 10 years early. Every pound you save is another pound that you can put towards your lifestyle during retirement. As we saw in Chapter 3 on budgeting, reducing your expenditure has the dual effect of freeing up more income now and reducing the amount you need to save to pay for your retirement. This assumes that you don't radically alter your spending habits once you stop work.

In this chapter, you will find a whole series of ideas to help you save money. These are designed to get your grey matter working so you can think of your own ways to reduce expenditure. More money saved means more money towards your early retirement plans.

> **More money saved means more money towards your early retirement plans.**

We also look at the more radical practice of 'extreme budgeting'. This is hardcore cost cutting, but can be a good way to get in the right frame of mind for longer-term savings.

Finally, we look at some of the ways in which you can save money on the investments and other financial products you buy.

Over 20 ways to spend less money

This is by no means an exhaustive list of ways to save money and cut back on your expenditure. Getting the best deal has almost become a sport in its own right in recent years. Just search for 'money saving' on the Internet to find plenty of websites where users discuss their money-saving tips and experiences.

Here are 27 different ways in which you can make a big difference to the amount of money that leaves your bank account each month.

1 **Eat out less.** Eating out in a restaurant or café is always more expensive than eating at home because you pay for the service and atmosphere. By eating out less, you can make those you do have more of a special occasion. As well as saving money, eating at home can lead to a healthier lifestyle because you can control what goes into the meals you prepare.

2 **Insist on having a water meter fitted.** Many water companies are starting to insist that homeowners have a water meter. If yours doesn't, you can ask the company to fit one. By having a water meter, you only pay for the water you use. Not having a water meter means paying the average water bill based on the size of your house. If you are part of a smaller household living in a bigger house, then that can mean you pay a lot more for water as you are also paying for water you are not actually using. When we asked for a water meter to be fitted, we saved around £25 a month – a big saving over time. It also makes you think a bit more about the water you *are* using, which is good for the environment.

3 **Drive an older car and keep it for longer.** Running a car is very expensive once you factor in insurance, petrol, tax and maintenance costs. Buying a new car and replacing it frequently is a sure-fire way to massively increase this item of expenditure. By buying a slightly older car you can reduce these costs. In the first three years of owning a new car, the value can plummet. By purchasing a car that is already over three years old, you can let somebody else pay for this depreciation. The value of your car will still go down, but it should fall at a lower rate from then on. Driving a slightly older car and owning it for longer can mean higher servicing

and repair costs but, compared to the initial depreciation associated with buying a new car, these are a drop in the ocean.

> In the first three years of owning a new car, the value can plummet.

4 **Take holidays at home, not abroad.** The cost of holidays – particularly if you have a family and are forced to go during the school holidays – can be incredibly high. This is one area of expenditure where you can make big savings. Young children, in particular, do not need expensive foreign holidays and will be just as happy with a week or two in the UK. For extremely low-cost holidays, try camping in the UK or Europe – the cost savings can be significant.

5 **Plan your meals in advance.** In our household, we write up a menu at the start of each week. Planning like this means that we can shop for the food we need rather than the food we think we'll need. Supermarkets are very clever when it comes to convincing shoppers to buy more than they need. As soon as you go through the doors of your local supermarket, you are bombarded with special offers and discounts to encourage you to buy more. If you don't think this is a problem, then take a long hard look at how much food you throw away in an average week. By planning your meals in advance, you can plan your food shopping in advance. This will allow you to ignore the special deals on offer and just buy what you need.

6 **Make a shopping list and stick to it.** As with creating a menu each week, writing a shopping list before you go to the shops will focus your mind on buying only those things that you need to buy. If you have a shopping list, then the special

offers and brightly coloured packaging of alternative items becomes far less tempting.

7 **Do all of your shopping online.** The best way to save money on your grocery shopping is to stay at home and shop using the Internet. This allows you to avoid the temptation of browsing for other goods. You can also use price comparison sites on the Internet to shop around for the best deals. The price differences for the same items from different supermarkets can be substantial. Checking for the best prices takes a few extra minutes of your time but this is time you have saved by not driving to the supermarket and standing in queues. The one drawback you might find with doing the grocery shopping online is the delivery charges. Many supermarkets have a minimum spending level before you get free home delivery. This can make it harder to shop around because you need to do all of your food shopping in one place. If this proves a problem for you, then choose the supermarket with the lowest overall prices and cheapest delivery charge. They all sell the same branded items anyway!

8 **Don't send your children to a private school.** Paying to send children to a private school is becoming more and more expensive. Over the past five years, the cost of private school fees has risen by over 40 per cent. This far exceeds the rate of price inflation for the other things we spend money on. The average cost of sending a child to a private school, as a day pupil, now stands at around £10,000 a year. While sending your child to a State school may not be completely free of charge (you still have to pay for uniforms and extra activities), it is significantly less expensive than the private school option.

9 **Review your insurance policies each and every year.** Your insurance policies represent some of the biggest opportunities for savings. When your car and home and contents policies

come up for renewal each year, you should see this as a good opportunity to shop around and save some money. The Internet has made it possible to obtain multiple insurance quotes by filling in a single enquiry form. Many insurance companies will also offer cheaper insurance premiums if you deal with them online rather than by telephone or post. When trying to save money on your insurance premiums, you should make sure the level of cover is the same with the new cover and you are not losing any benefits. This is one area where it pays to shop based on price and value.

10 **Don't join a gym.** Gym membership can be one of the most wasteful items of expenditure. I'm sure that we have all been there before. You join the gym with the best of intentions, possibly as part of a New Year's resolution to keep fit and healthy. The first few weeks (or even months!) are fantastic and you work out at the gym a number of times a week. Your membership starts to feel like great value for money. Then you hit a plateau. You find yourself going to the gym less frequently. All this time you are still paying the monthly membership fees and might even be locked into a 12-month contract. Instead of paying for expensive gym membership, find alternative ways to keep fit. Dust off that old bicycle in your garage or just go walking. The best exercise is free of charge and the money you save on gym membership can keep you kitted out in decent gear to make the most of it.

11 **Buy cheaper clothes.** If you like your designer labels, then buying cheaper clothes could represent a good cost-cutting opportunity for you. Consider using cheaper non-designer clothing to create the basis for your wardrobe and then dress this up a bit with a few designer items. The quality of designer and non-designer labels are often comparable anyway and nobody really cares what you are wearing as long as it is clean and ironed!

12 **Own brand, not a brand name.** Buying own brand goods from the supermarket can make a big difference to your expenditure. In a lot of cases, the own brand food is the same as the branded food, but in different packaging. Paying extra for flashy packaging is financial madness as it is the one part of the product that you will recycle or throw away! Branded food is often packaged in a way that makes it look more expensive or of a higher quality than the own brand alternatives. The best advice here is to try out the own brand products and do a taste test to compare them with the branded products that you would normally buy. In the majority of cases you will not be able to taste the difference, but buying the own brand ones could lead to a significant cost saving.

13 **Take out cash for your weekly budget and leave your cards at home.** This is a budgeting technique that works for my wife and I. We know how much our budget allows us to spend each week, so we withdraw that money in cash at the start of the week, then leave our debit and credit cards safely at home. This removes the temptation to buy unnecessary things and makes it easier to keep an eye on how much we are spending. Any leftover cash at the end of the week goes into savings.

14 **Switch utility provider.** It is possible to make big savings on your home utility bills if you are prepared to switch provider. There are price comparison sites on the Internet that will help you to find the most competitive deal for where you live and the amount of gas and electricity you consume. Switching your gas and electricity to one provider can also lead to savings. As with all items of expenditure, you should keep this under review and check it on at least an annual basis to make sure that your provider is still the most competitive. Don't have any concerns about chopping and changing utility provider on a regular basis. Threatening to move to another provider might actually encourage your existing provider to cut your bills.

15 **Swap toys with other families.** If you have a young family, then you can make a big cost saving by swapping toys with other parents you know. Toys are expensive and don't ever seem to last for long as children get older. By exchanging your toys for those more suitable for an older child you can keep your child entertained without forking out for expensive toys on a frequent basis. It also reduces the number of old toys that you have to find storage space for.

16 **Borrow books and films from the library.** Tell me honestly, when was the last time you went to your local library? I work right next door to our village library and cannot honestly remember the last time I went in there, yet I will happily visit our local video or book shop to spend my money. Libraries represent a good opportunity to save money if, like me, you read a lot of books and watch a lot of films.

17 **Watch less television.** Watching television is not only expensive, if you subscribe to a cable or satellite package, but also reduces the time you have available to make extra money and manage your personal finances. As a nation, we only spend an average of 60 minutes a week reviewing our finances, but over eight hours a week watching TV. Instead of watching television, you could read more books (borrowed from your library, of course!) or find innovative ways to earn extra money that can go towards your plans for early retirement. If you are a self-confessed television addict, then at least consider not watching the advertisements. In the past two years, I have not watched any adverts on TV and it has saved me a huge amount of time. By recording everything I want to watch and then skipping through the adverts, I cut down the amount of time I spend in front of the TV and I'm also less susceptible to falling for those marketing messages for things I don't need. Avoiding the adverts therefore has a double benefit.

18 **Leave the car at home.** Start making a habit of leaving the car at home when you need to go to places less than two miles away. The majority of car journeys in the UK are less than two miles long. If you walked or cycled all of these journeys, just think how much you could save each year on petrol and car maintenance costs. All of that extra exercise will also leave you feeling healthier and will give you more energy.

19 **Take a packed lunch to work.** How much do you spend on lunch each day? By making your own packed lunch and taking it to work, you could save a lot of money over the course of the year and a significant amount of cash over your working lifetime. Imagine that you spend £5 a day on your lunch. A lot of people I know spend more than that. If you assume that your packed lunch will cost you £1.50 a day to make, then that is a cost saving of £17.50 a week, £840 over an average working year and £33,600 over a forty-year working life.

20 **Wash your car by hand.** My local car wash charges around £5 a time to wash my car. Because I use my car a lot for business, I like to keep it looking clean, so tend to get it washed once a fortnight. That's £130 a year going to my local car wash for doing an easy job that I can probably do myself in the same amount of time it takes to drive there, sit in the car while it is being washed and drive home again.

21 **Grow your own vegetables.** I've tried this cost-cutting measure for the past two years with limited success. In the first year, I managed to harvest one courgette and this year all I had to show for my efforts was a small crop of potatoes and a few shallots. I will persevere as I think that this is one way to cut down on the weekly food bill and, at the same time, eat organic home-grown vegetables.

22 Cut your own hair. This one is a bit extreme as cost-cutting measures go, but worth considering if you have a simple hairstyle. For men, it makes real sense. My barber charges me £10 to cut my hair and I need to have it cut about once a month. That's £120 a year or almost £5000 over my working life. Alternatively, I could invest in a decent set of clippers for £20 and do it myself. The best thing about cutting your own hair is that it will grow back!

23 Stop drinking bottled water. Bottled water is a huge waste of money if you live in a first-world country with a clean drinking water supply. If you really can't stand the taste of tap water (and I concede that some people really don't like to drink it), then spend a few pounds on a water filter and a sports drinking bottle, like those used when cycling. Your investment in these two items will quickly be recovered as you will stop spending money every day on bottled water. In many cases, bottled water is from public drinking water supplies anyway. You are effectively paying for tap water!

24 Book your holiday at the right time. Conventional wisdom tells us to book our holiday at the very last minute to bag a bargain. This makes sense if you are reasonably flexible about where you stay and the times you travel. The alternative is to book your holiday incredibly early. If you book around 11 months before you want to go away, then you can snap up the discounts on offer for booking early. Booking early also has the added benefit of giving you plenty of time to save up and reduces the risk that you will put the holiday on a credit card.

25 Save your loose change. This is a great way to save money without even realising it. At the end of each day, put your loose change into a jar and promise not to touch it until the end of the month. Doing this will not have a major impact on your spending, but it will give you an extra £10 to £20 a month that you can put towards your early retirement plans.

26 Quit smoking. The cost savings associated with giving up smoking are substantial. A 20-a-day smoker can save almost £40 a week or £2000 in a year. There are other financial benefits from giving up smoking. Your life, health and home insurance will all become cheaper. Now that England has joined the rest of the UK with a smoking ban in enclosed public places, there has never been a better time to give up smoking.

27 Get rid of your home telephone. Do you really need to be paying line rental for a home telephone? If you have a mobile phone, then you can cheaply make and receive calls using that instead of paying for the costs associated with a home telephone. The rise in Voice over Internet Protocol (VoIP) technology means that you can also use your PC as a way to make telephone calls. This is particularly good if you have friends and relatives living overseas. We use our Internet connection to call friends and relatives in South Africa at zero cost.

Extreme budgeting

Cutting costs is one way to free up more of your income so that you can put it towards your plans for an early retirement. Another more radical way to cut expenditure is to indulge in a bout of 'extreme budgeting'.

I heard about extreme budgeting in an online article about a year ago. The article told the story of a man who spends one

It is a bit like crash dieting for your wallet.

month each year spending as little as possible. He sets himself the challenge of spending less each time he embarks on this month of extreme budgeting. It is a bit like crash dieting for your wallet.

Having a major financial detox for a month each year sounds like a great way of realising the wasteful nature of most expenditure. It is the money that we spend each month on, well, essentially nothing that reduces our ability to meet other financial objectives. After the cost of servicing debt, wasteful spending has the biggest impact on meeting plans for an early retirement. If you can spend an entire month not wasting any of your discretionary spending, then you will start to get into the habit of spending less in the future.

It's not just our discretionary spending that can be wasteful. Paying bills by direct debit or standing order can be a very efficient way of remembering to pay on time. Some service providers also offer a discount for customers who pay by direct debit. It is, however, very important to review all of your direct debits and standing orders on a regular basis as many of us completely forget to cancel direct debits or standing orders for things we no longer need. Also, with a growing number of organisations encouraging us to pay by direct debit, it is essential that you keep a close eye on the money automatically leaving your bank account each month. Remember, not all direct debits are monthly – some occur on a less frequent basis. These can sometimes be overlooked for longer, so carefully check your bank statements each month and account for every item of expenditure.

Slashing other costs

In addition to cutting back on your expenditure, you need to cut costs on everything in order to maximise your chances of retiring 10 years early. One of the main areas in which you can save a significant amount of money over the long term is the charges on your investments and other financial products.

As an independent financial adviser, I regularly review the market for my clients. It is always shocking to see the difference in price between the cheapest and most expensive products. For every type of financial product – pensions, investments, life assurance, mortgages – there is a massive difference between the cheapest and most expensive.

Here is my guide to making sure that you get the best deal every single time.

1 **Never buy a financial product from a tied agent.** If you are buying any financial product, then always do so based on an independent whole market comparison. Buying from a company that can only offer its own products is a sure-fire way to end up buying an uncompetitive product. Because the world of financial services changes so rapidly, the only way you can ensure best value is to use an independent financial adviser. Tied or multi-tied financial advisers might occasionally have a competitive product, but no single provider can ever hope to be the most competitive at all times.

2 **Always ask to see the comparison.** If you buy a financial product, you should always ask to see a copy of the research that has been conducted. Do not be surprised if your adviser did not recommend the absolute cheapest product. There are many factors that we take into account when recommending investments and other financial products. Price is an important factor, but so is financial strength, administration and the range of investment funds available. That said, if your adviser has recommended one of the more expensive products, you should be asking some serious questions about his or her motivation for doing so. A product with higher charges usually means higher levels of commission. If this seems to

be the only reason for the recommendation, then fire that adviser and get one who is better aligned with your best interests.

3 **Stop paying for active fund management.** This is a more radical suggestion that not every investment adviser feels entirely comfortable with. There have been studies that show active fund management – where a fund manager makes day-to-day decisions about how your money is invested – represents very poor value for money. Most fund managers fail to consistently beat the targets they set for themselves, yet you have to consistently pay fund management charges. The alternative to high charges for active management is to use passive or tracker investment funds. These aim to follow a particular investment market and do not require the same level of fund management involvement. The management charges are much lower as a result. Not every type of investment can be accessed using a tracker fund, but you should consider using one when it is available.

4 **Only pay for features that you use.** A lot of financial products come with extra bells and whistles that are only appropriate if you are a very sophisticated investor. A good example of this is the Self-Invested Personal Pension (SIPP). This allows policyholders to invest their pension funds in a very wide range of different investments, including company shares and commercial property. Because they offer this additional investment flexibility, they can be expensive. A cheaper alternative is a personal pension that offers access to a wide range of investment funds from different fund managers. These come in at a lower cost than a SIPP, yet offer almost as much investment choice.

5 **Get the service you pay for or stop paying for it.** The charges on most financial products include a commission for the person who sold it to you. This is fine as long as it is completely transparent and you get what you are paying for. For example,

if the annual management charge on an investment is paying 0.5 per cent of the fund value to the financial adviser each year, you have every right to expect to receive something in return. Depending on the size of your investment, this something might include a formal annual review of your plans, regular valuation statements and newsletters keeping you up to date with the investment markets. If you are not getting a good enough service, then consider moving to a new financial adviser who will do something in return for the money you are paying.

6 **Be a tart.** Most modern financial products have a charging structure that allows you to move to a new product or provider within a very short space of time. Two years is the usual maximum for which you would expect any penalties to apply, although some investments do carry longer penalty periods. If you can move to a new provider without penalty and somebody else in the market offers a more competitive contract, move! There is nothing wrong with being a 'rate tart' and constantly moving around to take advantage of the best offers. Most financial institutions provide poor terms to their existing policyholders in the hope that apathy will prevent them from leaving. Don't be one of those people who leaves their money languishing in an uncompetitive product simply because they can't be bothered to get better value elsewhere. If a better deal exists and you won't be penalised for moving out of your existing product, then the only thing stopping you is your commitment to getting a better deal.

A helping hand from the taxman

“George wrote Taxman, and I played guitar on it. He wrote it in anger at finding out what the taxman did. He had never known before then what could happen to your money.

Paul McCartney (1942–)

08

To paraphrase Benjamin Franklin, nothing is certain, except death and taxes. Tax can be a help as well as a hindrance, however, when it comes to your early retirement planning.

In this chapter, we will take a closer look at ways to legally reduce your tax bill. There is an important distinction here between the illegal evasion of tax and the perfectly legal avoidance of tax. As I don't want to encourage you to do anything that could get you into trouble with HM Revenue & Customs, the contents of this chapter will stick to the tried and tested legal forms of tax planning. However, you should still seek professional advice if you are unsure as to whether or not a certain course of action will get you into trouble tax-wise.

We also look at some of the tax incentives on offer for saving for your retirement. Where a helping hand is available from the taxman it makes sense to consider taking it. This sometimes results in restrictions, but, as long as you fully understand them, you can embrace tax relief with your arms wide open.

So, what's the problem?

Paying tax is an accepted fact of life. We might not like or enjoy paying tax but, like death, the payment of tax is inevitable. The problem with tax for early retirement planning is two-fold.

1 It reduces the amount of money you have available now to put towards your plans for an early retirement. If you can reduce the amount of tax you pay today, you will have more financial resources that you can use to realise your dreams of retiring 10 years early.

2 Tax continues to be paid once you have retired. Getting into the good habit of reducing your tax bill before you retire will make it easier to keep this up during retirement. Doing so

reduces the amount of money you need to maintain your lifestyle during retirement.

When it comes to retirement planning, there are three main types of tax to consider:

1 **Income tax.** When you earn money – in the form of a salary or income from investments – you have to pay income tax. This tax takes a percentage of what you earn and you receive what is left over. This is one of the commonest forms of tax and you are probably very familiar with how it works. In case you are in need of a quick refresher, it is a form of tax applied to different bands of earnings. For your salary, there are lower, basic and higher rate tax bands. The more you earn, the higher the rate of income tax on that part of your earnings. Income tax hits the highest earners the hardest. As a higher rate income tax payer, you have to pay 40 per cent tax on part of your earnings. Clearly this can have a major impact on your ability to save and invest in your early retirement. Later in this chapter we will look at some ways to reduce the impact of income tax for higher and basic rate income tax payers.

2 **Capital gains tax.** When you sell things, you sometimes have to pay tax on the difference between what you sold it for and what you paid for it in the first place. The difference between these two values is known as a capital gain. Capital gains tax is calculated by adding any relevant amount of capital gain to your income for that tax year to work out how much tax you need to pay. This means that capital gains tax is more expensive for higher earners who already pay higher rate income tax or people who are very close to paying higher rate income tax. This is a confusing type of tax because the way you calculate the actual capital gain is quite complicated. Later in this chapter we will look at some ideas for reducing any capital gains tax that you might have to pay.

3 **Inheritance tax.** Technically, this form of tax is not a problem

for you as it is only paid when you die. However, you might want to think about inheritance tax to save your children or other beneficiaries from paying unnecessary tax rather than in the context of it being a tax problem for you to solve for yourself. Your beneficiaries will have to pay inheritance tax at the rate of 40 per cent on the value of your assets over a certain threshold known as the nil rate band. From 6 April 2008, this nil rate band is £312,000 and it goes up each year at the start of the new tax year. This means that if you die and your estate is worth £500,000, your beneficiaries will have to pay inheritance tax of £75,000 (£500,000 less £312,000, multiplied by 40 per cent).

Evasion and avoidance

When it comes to tax planning, you need to be aware of these two important words.

■ **Evasion** means a criminal attempt to pay less tax than you owe. You should never evade tax because the penalties range from a severe telling off from the taxman (if you are very lucky!) to hefty fines and even time in prison.

■ **Avoidance** means using the law to reduce the amount of tax you owe. There is nothing wrong with tax avoidance and it should be used at every possible opportunity! Another form of tax avoidance is tax mitigation. Essentially this means the same thing, but tax experts apply a slightly different definition.

Understanding the difference between evasion and avoidance (or mitigation) is essential if you are going to be able to stay on the right side of the taxman and maximise your tax-planning opportunities.

How to pay less tax

The key to paying less tax is careful planning. By maximising any available allowances and making best use of tax relief, you can drastically reduce the amount of unnecessary taxes you pay each and every year. It is estimated that, in the UK, we waste £7.9 billion each year by not taking steps to reduce our tax payments. That is an average of £160 for every taxpayer.

The key to paying less tax is careful planning.

Here are 10 simple steps to help you reduce unnecessary tax payments. Less money wasted on tax means that more money can go towards fulfilling your dreams of an early retirement.

1 **Check your tax code.** Your tax code is used by your employer to work out how much tax should be deducted from your pay. If you have the wrong code, you could be paying too much or too little income tax each month. For most tax codes, you can simply multiply the number by 10 to find out how much income you can earn in a tax year before having to pay any income tax. This tax free allowance (called the personal allowance) is reduced by a number of factors and may be lower if you have additional employee benefits, such as a company car or private medical insurance. If you think that your tax code is incorrect, you should start by speaking to your employer and then to your local tax office.

2 **Use your ISA allowances.** Paying income tax on savings interest when you have not utilised your ISA allowances is wasteful and unnecessary. Everyone over 16 years old can contribute £3000 each tax year (£3600 from 6 April 2008) into a cash ISA. This allows you to earn interest without

being liabile for income tax. The headline rate of interest on the ISA account is the same as the interest you get to keep. As an added benefit, cash ISAs typically have better interest rates than ordinary bank or building society accounts.

3 **Make pension contributions.** Putting money into a personal pension is one of the easiest ways to get income tax relief. It is a particularly effective tax-planning strategy if you are a higher rate tax payer. Later in this chapter, I describe how tax relief on a pension works. Pension tax relief is one of the most generous forms of tax relief still available from the taxman. If you are planning for an early retirement and want to reduce your income tax bill, this is a very sensible way to pay less tax.

4 **Make a will.** Dying without a valid will in place – intestate – means that the Government decides who gets your money. It also means that you have no control over the amount of inheritance tax your beneficiaries will have to pay. Inheritance tax is often described as a voluntary tax because it can be largely reduced or even removed entirely with effective planning. The starting point for inheritance tax planning is getting a solicitor who specialises in estate planning to draw up a will for you. For a very small cost, you could save your children or other beneficiaries a massive tax bill in the future. Writing a will also gives you peace of mind that your wealth will be distributed in accordance with your wishes when you die. Don't put off writing a will – do it today.

5 **Use your capital gains tax allowance.** The first amount of capital gains that we make each tax year is completely free of tax. For the 2007/08 tax year, this annual exempt amount is £9200 and it increases each year. Even if you do not need to sell an investment in a tax year, you should consider selling something to make use of this capital gains tax exemption. If you do not use the exemption in one tax year,

it is wasted. Capital gains tax is one of the more complicated areas of tax planning. If you have various investments and are concerned about the amount of capital gains tax you will have to pay, do speak to a tax specialist, such as an accountant, who will be able to advise you.

6 **Give money to your partner.** If you are a higher rate tax payer and your spouse is a non-earner, you should consider putting assets into his or her name. For example, a higher rate tax payer with £50,000 in a savings account earning 5.5 per cent interest will have to pay £1100 in income tax on that money each year. If that person's spouse was a non-earner, he or she could immediately save £1100 by putting the savings into the spouse's name. This is a simple and effective tax planning strategy. Unfortunately, it is often overlooked by people in search of more complicated and adventurous ways to save tax.

7 **Give money to your children.** Because children also have a tax-free allowance each tax year, it can be effective to gift money to them. Be aware that if this generates over £100 a year in interest, the tax liability stays with the parent. Based on an interest rate of 5.5 per cent, this means that you can give them capital of up to £1818 before the tax has to be assessed on your tax position. This only allows you to save a small amount of income tax, but every little helps.

8 **Rent out a room.** If you rent out a room in your house to a lodger, you can receive up to £4250 a year in rent completely free of tax. This is known as the 'rent a room' scheme. As well as the tax-free nature of the rent, it means that additional income can be put towards your plans for an early retirement. You might even consider renting out a room after you retire to supplement your income in retirement.

9 **Submit your tax return and pay your tax on time.** Over a million tax returns a year are returned late. If you don't send in your tax return on time (by 31 January), you will receive an

automatic £100 fine. Plan in advance and start working on your tax return as soon as you can after the end of the tax year. Check and double-check the figures you put down on your tax return to ensure that they are correct. Once you know how much tax you have to pay, make sure that you pay it on time. If you don't pay your tax on time, you have to pay interest charges.

10 Use an accountant. If you have particularly complicated tax affairs, such as multiple sources of income or capital gains, then the cost of an accountant will be worthwhile as he or she can make you big savings. Look for an accountant who will take a proactive approach to tax planning. Many accountants are very good historians and can produce an excellent set of accounts, but they don't do much to help you save tax in the future. The best accountants are historians who also help you plan for the future. The most effective way to find a good accountant is to ask for a referral from friends, family or colleagues. If they have had a good experience with their accountant they will be more than happy to tell you.

How does tax relief on pensions work?

Pensions are probably the most tax-friendly form of investment for retirement planning. They are tax-friendly in a number of different ways.

When you pay money into a pension plan, you get tax relief on that contribution. This tax relief comes in two parts. Depending on how much income tax you pay, you might be entitled to one

> Pensions are probably the most tax-friendly form of investment for retirement planning.

or both parts. The first part is the basic rate income tax relief. This is added directly to the pension fund to increase the amount of your contribution that is invested. As basic rate income tax is due to drop to 20 per cent on 6 April 2008, we will work on that basis. For example, if you contributed £100 to a personal pension, you would have an extra £25 added directly to your pension fund. A full £125 would then be available to invest in your chosen investment funds.

If you are a higher rate income tax payer, you can also reclaim the difference between the basic and higher rates of income tax. From 6 April 2008, this difference will be a further 20 per cent. On the same £100 contribution, this means that you can reclaim an extra £25 tax relief (20 per cent of £125). This money is usually paid back to you when you submit your tax return. You just need to remember to tell the taxman how much you paid into pensions during that tax year.

The money invested inside a pension wrapper is also subject to quite friendly tax treatment. Any growth or income on money inside a pension fund is free of tax. There is a slight exception to this statement as it is not longer possible to reclaim the tax paid on the income from company shares. Apart from this anomaly, the rest of the investment returns within your pension fund are free of tax.

When you decide to take retirement benefits from your pension fund, there is a further bit of friendliness from the taxman. You are allowed to take up to 25 per cent of the value of your pension fund as a cash sum, which is completely free of tax. This cash sum is known as the 'pension commencement lump sum'. It used to be called 'tax-free cash', which was a much more descriptive name! Any income generated from your pension fund is, unfortunately, subject to income tax.

The final tax-friendly treatment of pension funds happens if you die before you take any benefits. In this unfortunate circumstance, your entire pension fund is paid to your partner, children or any other beneficiary completely free of tax. This happens because the value of your pension fund is not included in your estate for the purposes of calculating inheritance tax.

Tax and investments

When you invest money outside of a tax-efficient wrapper, you will need to pay tax on the returns. You will have to pay income tax on the investment income (such as dividends from company shares or rental income from property) and capital gains tax if the value of your investment has gone up when you come to sell it.

If you can reduce the amount of tax you pay on your investments, you can maximise the returns. It makes sense, therefore, to pay as little tax as possible by structuring your investments in the most tax-efficient manner. The following ideas for investment tax planning assume that you have already used up any tax-efficient investment options open to you.

1 **Invest offshore.** Squirrelling your money away in the Cayman Islands or Barbados to pay less tax has always sounded quite mysterious and a bit devious. The reality of offshore investment is quite different. It has become a perfectly acceptable tax-planning tool, used not just by ultra-high net worth investors but also plenty of everyday people planning for their retirement. Investors who keep their money offshore (essentially invested outside of the UK) do so to defer the payment of tax rather than not pay any tax at all. By delaying the timing of the tax payment, it is possible to save money because the investment growth is calculated based on the non-taxed return (known as gross rollup). Deferring the payment of tax also makes it possible to plan carefully for the time when you *do* pay the tax. If you can reduce your other

income for a tax year and then bring the investment back into the UK, you are likely to pay a lot less than you would under other circumstances. For all the advantages of offshore investments for tax planning, however, they do remain quite expensive in comparison to the onshore alternatives. Any tax savings can be largely eaten up by additional charges. There are also issues of financial security that you need to consider when investing your money outside of the UK. The important thing to remember with offshore investing is that you will end up having to pay tax at some point in the future.

2 **Use a life assurance company investment.** Life assurance companies offer different investment wrappers and one of the most interesting from a retirement and tax-planning perspective is the investment bond. This allows you to invest a capital sum in a range of different investment options. Tax is paid on these investments, but it is paid within the life assurance fund, depending on the type of investment. If you take money out of this investment, you will not have any further tax to pay if you are a basic rate or non-tax payer. Higher rate tax payers will have to pay additional tax if their investments have grown, but it is possible to delay the payment of this tax if you stick to the rules. You are able to withdraw up to 5 per cent of the original investment each year without any immediate liability to tax. This means that if you invested £50,000, you could withdraw up to £2500 for each complete year that money was invested. This withdrawal is really a return of your original capital rather than 'income', which is why the tax can be deferred until later, but this sort of investment can be set up to provide a regular stream of capital withdrawals that appear to be just like a tax-free investment income. Some unscrupulous financial advisers like to recommend these investments because they can pay very high levels of commission. If your financial adviser is recommending that you invest your money in a life assurance investment bond, you should make sure that you understand his or her reasons for doing so. Also, check to see which other

alternatives your adviser considered for you before making the recommendation. This sort of investment is particularly attractive for higher rate tax payers who are investing their tax-free cash sum when they come to take pension benefits. It allows them to convert that cash into 'income' and delay the eventual payment of any tax for up to 20 years.

3 **Sell some investments each year.** The annual capital gains tax exemption provides a very good tax-planning tool for investors who have already used up their annual ISA allowance. By selling some investments that have gone up in value each tax year, you could make use of the annual exemption and ensure that it is not wasted. If you assume an annual investment growth of 10 per cent, you could safely invest around £90,000 in non-tax-efficient investments and not have to worry about capital gains tax if you sold your investments each year. Rules are in place to prevent you from getting any tax benefit from selling and repurchasing the same investments within a 30-day timeframe, but there is nothing to stop you from buying a similar investment or from giving the sale proceeds to your spouse and then he or she buying the same investments. You should also make use of your partner's capital gains tax exemption if you are married. Moving investments between married couples does not create a capital gains tax liability, so you can do this and then allow your spouse to sell the investments. All of the investment growth is then assessed against his or her annual exemption and tax rate. The main drawback of this approach to capital gains tax planning is that you miss out on what is known as taper relief. This is a form of tax relief you get when you hold on to investments for a long period of time. You need to do so for at least three years to get any taper relief and the benefit of taper relief increases each year up to the tenth year, when you get the maximum taper relief of 60 per cent.

4 Don't keep company shares in an ISA. It is no longer possible for an ISA investment manager to reclaim the tax already paid on dividends (income) from UK company shares. For this reason, it does not make sense to use your ISA allowance to invest in UK company shares if you are a basic rate tax payer. There is still some advantage for a higher rate tax payer who does not have to pay any additional income tax on the dividend income. Instead of using up your ISA allowance on investments in company shares, consider using it to invest in fixed interest securities or property funds. The returns from these are completely free of tax within an ISA so you get the maximum benefit.

5 Invest in venture capital. An investment in a venture capital trust (VCT) attracts some very good tax breaks. VCTs are a very tax-efficient way of investing money. An investment in a VCT has income tax relief, tax-free income and capital gains tax relief. However, they are complicated investments and can be very high risk. VCTs were first introduced in 1995 and are designed to encourage private investors to invest in smaller companies. An investment in a VCT is riskier because the companies may go out of business. When you invest your money in a VCT, you get income tax relief of 30 per cent of the amount you invest. This means that a £10,000 investment results in a £3000 tax rebate. You have to hold on to the investment for at least five years to keep this tax relief, but any dividends paid back to you by the VCT are free of tax and there is no capital gains tax to pay when you sell your VCT investment. Because these are higher-risk investments, it is sensible to only invest in them if you are prepared to wait for the longer term before getting your money back.

Staying on track

" I am a goal setter and I set more goals every day.
I keep lists of goals in my office to stay on track.

Kiana Tom (1965–)

09

Once you make the decision to retire 10 years early and put your plans in place, it is important to stay on track.

Setting goals and then sticking to them is the most powerful way to ensure long-term success. When I set a long-term goal, I know that it will only happen if I simultaneously set a series of shorter-term goals. These milestones are what keep me on track and motivated to succeed with my long-term goals.

Knowing that you are making progress with your plans is a good motivator. Finding out that you are not keeping pace with your plans along the way gives you the opportunity to catch up, which has to be better than finding you have a lot to do some way down the line. There is nothing negative about regularly reviewing the progress of your early retirement plans.

> There is nothing negative about regularly reviewing the progress of your early retirement plans.

This chapter is all about staying on track. We start by looking at how much you actually need to save to retire. We also discuss how to measure your performance against predetermined targets, known as benchmarks.

How to conduct a thorough annual review of your plans for an early retirement and keep your financial paperwork well organised is also covered.

How much will you need to retire?

That's the million dollar question. Determining how much you will need to save in order to retire early is the essential starting point. Until you can establish the answer to this question you cannot work out how much you need to save or invest each year. Until you know, it is difficult, if not impossible, to monitor your progress.

The answer depends on a whole range of factors, including how much your expenditure is likely to be during retirement and what you can actually afford to save now.

The rule of thumb used to be to take two-thirds of your earnings at the time you planned to retire and make that your target retirement income. To do this you need to take your earnings today and escalate them each year in line with your assumptions about future earnings growth.

Let's assume that you are 32 years old and want to retire when you are age 55 – in 23 years' time. If you earn a salary of £30,000 today and assume that your earnings will grow at 4 per cent a year, that means a predicted salary of just under £74,000 a year when you are 55 years old. Two-thirds of £74,000 is just over £49,000 a year.

You need to keep a close eye on these assumptions as you get older. Your earnings might increase at a faster or slower pace than the 4 per cent a year you have assumed. If real life turns out to be different from your assumptions, then you need to make adjustments.

Rather than start with the two-thirds of salary at retirement formula, it makes more sense to first look at your likely expenditure during retirement. Peruse your current budget and decide which items will stop, reduce, stay the same or increase when you retire. Apply price inflation to these current numbers to

> Rather than start with the two-thirds of salary at retirement formula, look at your likely expenditure during retirement.

work out what they will be when you plan to retire. This should give you a fairly accurate idea of your likely expenditure requirements when you come to retire.

It is fairly typical for the gap between your income and expenditure to close as you get older and move into retirement. This can be dangerous because any unexpected expenditure (replacing your car or needing to buy a new boiler, for example) can lead to fairly instant financial misery.

Later in your life, you might experience a very comfortable level of excess income each month. Because earnings typically increase at a faster rate than price inflation, it is not unusual for this income/expenditure gap to continue to grow during your working life.

When you get into your 40s and 50s, you will probably be enjoying your peak earning years. At the same time, your expenditure on items such as your mortgage and funding education for your children may have stopped. More income and less expenditure will lead to a much larger amount of expendable income.

Making sense of these numbers

Once you have established a likely annual expenditure figure in retirement, you need to 'capitalise' it. This means that you need to convert an annual figure into a lump sum. Doing this helps you to work out how much wealth you need to build between now and your target date.

The way to turn an annual figure into a capital amount is to apply a conversion rate. This conversion rate is the amount of income you think you will be able to get from a capital sum. For example, if you could get 5 per cent income from your capital, you would use a conversion factor of 5 per cent.

Let's assume that you need £30,000 a year when you retire. If you could get an income of 5 per cent a year, you would need a lump sum of £600,000 as 5 per cent of £600,000 is £30,000 a year. If you could get a higher level of income than 5 per cent you would need less capital. A 6 per cent income rate would require you to accumulate £100,000 less in your retirement plans. If, on the other hand, you could only get a lower level of income, you would need more money. This is because a 4 per cent income rate, say, would require £750,000 to produce the same £30,000 a year income.

A number of different things will influence the number you decide to use to turn your projected annual expenditure into a capital sum.

1 **How much risk you are willing to take with your money.** As we saw in Chapter 6, to net a higher return on your money means that you have to take more investment risk. If you are a high-risk investor who is prepared to accept shorter-term losses, then you can opt for a higher number. A more cautious investor should go for a smaller number.

2 **Wanting capital growth as well as income.** If you plan to just use the capital you build up to provide income alone, this puts less pressure on your capital than if you want it to grow as well. If you want capital growth as well as income during retirement, you should choose a small income rate or your goals for achieving capital growth will be difficult to reach.

3 **Your health.** Poor health can lead to shorter life expectancy, which means that your money will not need to last for as long. You can safely choose a higher income figure because you can afford to erode the value of your capital. In very simple terms, there is less risk that your money will run out before you die. That is why poor health often leads to much higher annuity rates when people come to convert their pension capital into an income. The annuity provider can afford to offer a higher annuity rate because the company doesn't expect to have to pay the income for as long as it

would need to if you were in good health. The same rule applies to smokers as well.

4 Interest rates when you retire. The rate of interest when you retire will have a big influence on the likely level of income you can generate from your capital. A higher rate of interest means that you can safely generate a higher level of income and that you will need less capital. Unfortunately, it is very difficult to predict what interest rates will look like over the longer term. To be on the safe side, you should assume a lower rate of interest. If interest rates turn out to be higher, then at least you will have more income than you actually require.

Now what?

Once you have worked out the sort of capital sum you need to build up in time for your planned early retirement date, you can start working towards it. Use some more realistic assumptions about how much your money might grow in value each year.

Work out how much you can comfortably afford to save towards your retirement plans each year. Will that be enough to meet your early retirement planning goals? Remember that you are likely to be able to save more towards your early retirement as you get older and your earning powers increase.

You should also bear in mind that any initial debt reduction you manage to achieve in the early years of your plan also count towards your retirement plans. It might be hard to see the impact any debt reduction has on your plans for an early retire-ment, but every £1 of debt you clear today will save you money in the future. By doing this you are reducing your capital target and freeing up more of your financial resources to put towards your early retirement plans in the future. For this reason, clearing debt is as important, if not more important, than building up massive pension or investment funds.

Clearing debt is as important, if not more important, than building up massive pension or investment funds.

Monitoring your progress

When you are making plans to retire 10 years early, it is important to be able to compare your own progress against that of others. That means you need to set benchmarks. A benchmark is commonly used when investing money as a way to compare different portfolios.

There are several different ways in which you can benchmark the performance of your early retirement plans.

1 **Relative performance.** By measuring your performance against what the rest of the investment market is doing, you can compare the relative performance of your plans. This means that if the stock market has gone up 10 per cent over the past year and your early retirement plans have only gone up by 8 per cent, things are not looking good. If your own early retirement plans had gone up by 12 per cent you might feel a bit happier. Using relative performance is just as important when the stock market or other investments have fallen in value. If, for example, the stock market dropped in value by 6 per cent, you might not feel too bad if your own portfolio had only dropped in value by 3 per cent. The relative performance would look good. So, relative performance is all about making more money than the rest of the market when things are going up in value and losing less money than everyone else when things are going down. Not everyone feels good about losing less money than the rest of the market, so, for that reason, a second benchmark is often used as well.

2 Absolute performance. This sets a positive growth target for each year. An absolute return is an investment return greater than zero. The way that we would normally construct an absolute benchmark is to add up three different numbers:

- we look at the charges levied on your investments
- we take the estimated rate of price inflation for the year ahead
- we add in the amount of investment growth you expect to get.

By combining these three figures, you can set a target for the rate your portfolio has to grow each year to produce a total return that you feel comfortable with. It may be difficult to meet absolute return targets like this each and every year. It is often a good idea to take a three- or five-year view of an absolute return target. That way a poor stock market performance in one year can be put in the context of better performance in subsequent years.

Your annual financial review

One of the most important things that you can do to keep your plans for early retirement on track is conduct a thorough annual review of your personal finances.

As a financial planner, this is the sort of thing I get involved with on a frequent basis. I have a number of clients who pay me to produce a comprehensive annual review of their financial planning each and every year. They still have a great deal of input into these plans, but all of the ground work – gathering data and analysis – is conducted for them.

It was only quite recently that I decided to add my own name to the list. Before then I had a good grasp of our family's own financial planning, but nothing formal was in place. Since I did this, we've been in a much stronger financial position. It is easier to get a snapshot of where we are in financial terms.

> The real benefit of an annual financial review is the ability to track your progress.

The real benefit of an annual financial review is the ability to track your progress each year. Knowing how much (or how little!) progress you have made in financial terms over the past 12 months is a very powerful motivator to keep going and make more progress.

Once the first review report has been created, it is then incredibly easy to simply update it each year with the current figures. This means that you don't always have to wait for a whole year to elapse before you produce a new review.

How to conduct an annual review

Conducting an annual review of your financial plans is fairly simple. The secret is to have a structure and make sure that you stick to that same structure each year. Doing so means that you have to put a bit of effort into getting the first report up to a high standard, but then it is fairly easy to produce a new review each year.

The reports my family and I produce use the following simple structure.

1 Introduction and objectives. This page sets the scene for the rest of the review. It is a place to state the purpose of having

> Have a structure and make sure that you stick to that same structure each year.

a financial plan. When we write down our objectives, they are more likely to happen. It is also the place to make any general comments about the plan and the review. Putting these comments near the front of the review report makes it easy to refer to them at a glance in the future.

2 Assumptions. If any assumptions are used in the review, it is important to write them down. Simply list any assumptions that have been used, along with the rates that have been assumed. It is important to keep this part of the review near the start as parts of the rest of the review are likely to rely on some of these assumptions. You can also compare the assumptions you are making this year with those made in any earlier reviews.

3 Assets. This page is a summary of the current value of your cash, investments, pension plans and property. It offers an at-a-glance list of your different assets and their current values. You should also make a brief note here to compare your total assets this year with those in previous years.

4 Liabilities. Any debt or upcoming one-off expenditure should be recorded here. Keep your short-term and long-term debt on separate parts of the page. Detail is really important for this page as you should be listing the amount of debt outstanding, the interest rate, the final repayment date and how much you are currently paying each month for the debt. Just like your assets, you should compare your current liabilities with those recorded in previous years.

5 Income and Expenditure. From a budgeting perspective, this is possibly the most important page of the review report. It is designed to be a snapshot of how much you earn, how much tax you pay and how much you spend during the course of the year. Detail is quite important here as well as making a comparison between your actual and budgeted expenditure. It is a good way to see just how much you spend on what. Until you see your annual income and expenditure summary, it can be difficult to establish just where your money went each month! You should also make reference on this page to income and expenditure totals for previous years.

6 **Personal risk management.** Because we have a young family, this section of our annual review report is very important. You may or may not choose to include it every year, but it makes real sense to review personal risk management from time to time. On this page we summarise any life assurance or other financial protection policies we have in place. We also run through some simple scenarios to determine what the financial impact on our family would be if any of them were to occur. These scenarios include death, contracting a serious illness and not being able to work for a length of time because of accident or illness. By testing your finances like this, it is easier to identify any gaps in your life assurance or protection policies.

7 **Retirement planning.** For the person following a RTYE plan, this is one of the most important parts of the review. It is the page where you compare your plans and targets with your progress. To do this, you can bring together the information you have collated for the rest of the review.

8 **Other issues.** This is a page we include in our annual review to capture any other relevant information. In previous years, we have used it to discuss issues such as making a will and appointing a guardian for our child. It is effectively a miscellaneous page, but including it in the review report will hopefully prompt you to consider financial issues that might be missing from the rest of the review structure. If you have nothing to add to this page, then leave it blank, but leave it in the review report so you remember to include it next year.

9 **Plan of action.** Your review should finish with a brief statement about what steps you need to take to stay on track over the next 12 months. Make a list, with the most urgent action points at the top. Included within the list should be a note to conduct the review all over again in 12 months' time. If the

review throws up some serious financial problems, then you might want to review things again in three months' time to keep on top of things until the situation improves.

What to keep and what to dump

One of the hardest tasks when you are monitoring your progress is trying to decide which paperwork you need to keep. Clients often arrive at our offices with carrier bags full of financial paperwork. The ability to sort through these and condense several bags' worth into one small folder is clearly very valuable!

> Keep any original policy documents and the most recent valuation statement for every financial policy.

The basic rule is to keep any original policy documents and the most recent valuation statement for every financial policy. When an update valuation statement arrives in the post, you should use this as a prompt to throw away the last one. Before you throw it away, though, conduct a quick comparison to make sure that the new statement looks accurate and reflects what has changed in the past 12 months.

When you come to throw financial paperwork away, be very careful. Identity theft is becoming a growing worldwide problem and those bits of paper can be very attractive to criminals who make their living from your personal data. If anything you are getting rid of contains personal data, you should ensure that it is well shredded before it is recycled or thrown away. The less environmentally conscious among you may even want to dispose of your old financial papers in a bonfire.

The alternatives to early retirement

> Retirement at 65 is ridiculous. When I was 65 I still had pimples.
>
> George Burns (1896–1996)

10

> **Many of the people I speak to plan to never retire.**

The idea of early retirement doesn't suit everyone. Many of the people I speak to plan to never retire. They want to continue to work until they drop and enjoy every minute of it. This is particularly true of business owners who hope to keep businesses going that they've started up or inherited, for example.

The same goes for many employees. Continuing to make an important contribution to society is a powerful motivation for working past the traditional retirement age of 65.

Other people want to keep working, but make changes to their lifestyle at the same time. Rather than working five (or more!) days a week, they want to experience a more even work–life balance. I also speak to people who want to swap their career for something completely different. Very often that means a move away from a profession to a vocation or possibly even charitable work.

Our ideas about retirement are all very different. Fortunately, the RTYE plan can work for anyone, regardless of their ambitions for the timing of what we traditionally call retirement. By refocusing the plan on your own personal objectives, it is possible to gain very real benefits from following the ideas set out in this book.

> **The RTYE plan can work for anyone.**

This chapter is all about working for longer, but making those extra years really count. We also take a look at the ways in which you can defer taking State and private pensions if you decide to continue to work rather than retire.

Out of the blue

Sometimes early retirement is forced on us. Ill health and redundancy can strike without warning. Both can remove the option of working later in life.

A study in the US suggests that over 20 per cent of all people who retire are forced to do so earlier than they expected, either as a result of serious ill health or redundancy (Sun Life Financial, 'Forced retirement survey', December 2006). Of these, the majority said that their retirement plans were adversely affected. That's hardly surprising if the length of time you thought you still had left to plan for a financially secure lifestyle in retirement is suddenly and unexpectedly cut down to nothing.

A sudden redundancy can affect more than just your financial plans for retirement. Our jobs often define who we are as people. To lose a senior position or a job where a particular expertise was required can often make people feel like they are worthless, that they have lost their place in society. It can be a powerful shock that distracts us from our plans for retirement.

Aiming to retire 10 years early gives you choice and acts as a powerful defence in the face of ill health or redundancy – far more

> **Aiming to retire 10 years early gives you choice and acts as a powerful defence in the face of ill health or redundancy.**

than doing nothing and hoping for the best. Follow a plan to retire early. It will put you in a strong financial position and then the impact of either of these events can be more easily shrugged off.

Rather than being forced into finding another job if made redundant or returning to work quickly before fully recovering from a serious illness, you could put yourself in the financial position of having choice.

When it comes to retirement planning, choice is the main motivator. The choice as to whether or not you will relocate when your employer moves to a new office or can spend more time with your grandchildren when they are born. By planning now, you can have more choice in the future.

Why not aim to retire 10 years early with the intention of continuing to work? If you decide to do this and can continue working, then your financial position when you do come to retire will look extremely positive. If the worst does happen and you are forced to stop working, at least you will have built sufficient assets to see you through. It's a winning situation, regardless of what happens to you and your prospects for future employment.

What happens if you do nothing?

Doing nothing is always a valid option to consider when you have to make a decision. In fact, many decision makers use 'do nothing' as the first option to consider and then compare the alternatives to the outcome of total inaction. It's a good starting point to consider when thinking about retirement planning.

Deciding to do nothing when it comes to retirement planning is likely to mean that you end up like other people. In fact, doing nothing means that you could fall into one of the following groups identified in some research conducted by Prudential (Retirement Index, 21 June 2006):

- the 14 per cent of retired people in the UK who live on less than £5000 a year
- the 38 per cent who live on less than £10,000 a year
- the 53 per cent who live on less than £15,000 a year.

In fact, the average retirement income in the UK is £13,200 a year, which is only £1100 each month. In some areas of the UK, it is much lower than this. The area with the lowest average retirement income is Yorkshire, with an average income of £10,500 (£875 per month). Those in London are typically the best off, with an average income in retirement of £16,900 a year, but they may have higher living expenses as well.

These low levels of income mean that a lot of retired people have to cut back on their expenditure during retirement. Around two-thirds of retired people admit to having reduced their outgoings as a result of their lower income in retirement. Keep in mind that it is often the luxury items, including holidays and entertainment, that have to be cut out of the budget when income is reduced on retirement.

So, doing nothing is a valid option for your retirement planning. Doing nothing may also be what you find yourself doing during your retirement if your expenditure has to be severely pruned as a result of a lower than expected income.

Making the extra years count

If you decide to keep working past your normal retirement age, those extra years in employment can go a very long way towards ensuring that you have a comfortable lifestyle in retirement. Later in life, we tend to be able to put more money towards our retirement plans because of the following factors.

- **We earn more.** Earnings tend to increase with age because we are more experienced and tend to hold more senior positions as we get older. This increased earning capacity means that more income can be invested in your plans for retirement.

■ **We have less expenditure.** By the time we hit the age of 65, our mortgages are usually paid off and we are free of debt. Often our children have finished in full-time education and (hopefully) flown the nest to set up their own homes.

It's the combination of these two factors that means we can often put more money towards our plans for retirement as we get older than is possible earlier on in our lives. The only disadvantage of trying to build a bigger retirement fund at this time of life is the lack of time we have left in which to save.

When you start saving towards your retirement at an early age, there is lots of time for your wealth to grow. Because it will be invested for a longer time, the impact of compound investment growth causes it to grow at a relatively fast rate each year. When there is limited time before full retirement, the effects of compound investment growth are less beneficial.

You can still make every penny count at this stage, but it won't get the same helping hand from investment returns that your money did when you were younger.

Maximising State pension benefits

A good starting point, if you are thinking about maximising various pension benefits, is your State pension. It becomes payable at the age of 65 for men and 60 for women. In fact, for women, the State pension age is going to increase to 65 as well. It goes up in steps between 2010 and 2020, so, depending on your date of birth, you could have a State pension age of anywhere between 60 and 65.

The State pension age is unlikely to remain at 65 years old for very long once these changes have been made. The Government

> **The State wants you to work for longer before you can start drawing a pension.**

is proposing that we should all retire later. This means that the State pension age will go up a bit more, from 65 to 68, in stages, between 2024 and 2044. This should send a clear message to those hoping that the State will look after them during retirement. The State wants you to work for longer before you can start drawing a pension.

There is some good news hidden away in these proposed changes. To get a full basic State pension, you have to have worked for a certain length of time. This time in work is known as 'qualifying years' and reflects the amount of time that you have been making National Insurance contributions. Currently, men have to have worked and made these contributions for 44 years and women for 39 years in order to get the maximum basic State pension.

The new proposals plan to reduce the number of qualifying years so that, if you retire from April 2010, you will only need 30 qualifying years in order to receive a full basic State pension. Women who take time away from work to raise children or look after disabled relatives can count this time towards their qualifying years. The new system should make it much easier for more people to build an entitlement to the full basic State pension.

When you are planning your retirement benefits, it always makes sense to request a State pension forecast from The Pension Service, part of the Department for Work and Pensions. This is free of charge and will show you two important things.

1 How much State pension entitlement you already have. This number means that, if you stop working today, that is the amount you are likely to get when you retire.

2 A projection, which assumes that you will continue to work until the State pension age.

Knowing both of these numbers is an important planning step and you can use these projections as a basis for the rest of your retirement planning.

Deferring your pension benefits

When you get to whatever counts as a normal retirement age, you have a number of choices about what to do with your pension benefits. If you have made the decision to keep on working, then you do not necessarily need to start drawing an income from your pension.

Your State pension

When your State pension becomes payable, you don't actually have to take it. If you want, you can defer this benefit for as long as you want. At the end of the deferred period – which must last at least 12 months if you want a lump sum – you are then entitled to either a lump sum or higher weekly pension payments. Both the lump sum and higher weekly payments are taxable.

The lump sum is calculated by adding up the State pension benefits that you would have received and applying an interest rate of 2 per cent above the Bank of England base rate. If you take the lump sum option, then you start to receive your State pension at the ordinary rate.

The main drawback associated with deferring your State pension is the risk of death. If you do pass away before you claim the lump sum or enhanced State pension, you (well, actually, your family) receive nothing. This makes deferring your State pension a bit of a gamble as you get older.

Of course, you might take the view that you could simply accept the pension benefit and invest it wisely until you needed the money. You could do this in the hope of getting better returns than those on offer from the State and with the knowledge that the money would at least go to your family if you died earlier than expected. For most people, this is probably the more sensible option.

Private pensions

Since April 2006, the new pension rules have meant that it is possible to take the maximum permitted cash from your pension fund, but then not take any income. This option is particularly attractive for people who wish to pay off certain debts, like a mortgage, but continue working and earning a salary for a certain period of time.

At this stage, you might be wondering why anybody would turn down a pension income and delay it until some time in the future. In fact, there is usually a strong mathematical argument for taking the money today rather than later, so, under normal circumstances, it is the best thing to do. However, if you continue to work and are paid a salary after your normal retirement age, you might be subject to a higher rate of tax on the salary and pension income than before. Then, putting off receiving your pension income until a point when you don't have any other tax to pay *is* sensible from a financial planning perspective.

Working *and* retiring

The alternative to delaying your pension benefits is to keep working and start drawing a pension income. With hopefully fewer financial liabilities at this stage of your life, the double benefit of a salary *and* a pension income could make you a very wealthy individual. While you will probably end up paying a higher amount of tax, the extra income could be invested for the future.

Since the UK pension rules were updated in April 2006, it has been possible to take pension benefits from an occupational pension plan and keep working. This wasn't allowed under the 'old' rules. Then, in order to take your occupational pension benefits, you had to quit your job. This created the crazy situation of people resigning on their 65th birthday and then being rehired shortly afterwards in a slightly different role.

A strategy that we often discuss with our clients is that of recycling some of their income as new pension contributions. By using any surplus income from pensions to make *fresh* pension contributions, you can effectively achieve the following benefits.

- **Cancel out the income tax.** You will pay income tax on the pension income you receive, but get income tax relief on the contribution. This leads to a broadly neutral income tax position on the extra income.

- **Build up a new source of tax-free cash for the future.** Your recycled pension contributions will create a new pension fund and you will be able to take up to a quarter of the value of that fund as tax-free cash when you decide to take benefits in the future.

- **Improve the death benefits position.** The new pension fund you start to build can be passed to your partner or beneficiaries free of tax if you die before taking benefits from it. If you are drawing an income from an unsecured pension or in receipt of income from an annuity, this is a positive virtue of recycling the income.

You can pay up to 100 per cent of your earnings into a pension plan, assuming that you are under the age of 75. Even if you have no earnings, but are in receipt of excess income from a pension, you can pay up to £3600 into your pension each tax year.

Your early retirement checklist

> I've got the checklist; I'm making sure that we're doing everything on time; I'm making the calls to the ground.

Duane G. Carey, astronaut (1957–)

11

Here we go – the retire 10 years early plan condensed into a single chapter. Use what you have read in the rest of the book to make this early retirement checklist a reality. This chapter is more than just a summary – it is a step-by-step action plan checklist that you can use straight away. It's a super-summary of the entire contents of this book, designed to spur you into action right now.

The ideal early retirement plan is very personal. You should tailor this checklist to your needs and create your own. Make this plan to retire 10 years early your own. Think through how to strike a healthier balance between work and life at a younger than average age.

Here are the points you have to cover to make your early retirement plan a roaring success. Good luck!

1 **Make the decision to retire 10 years early.** If you don't make a clear decision to retire 10 years early, it is unlikely to happen. Make a commitment to an early retirement and write it down somewhere you will see it on a regular basis. When I write down my goals, I find that they are more likely to happen. This isn't earth-shattering science, just the power of a written reminder of what you are planning to achieve. I know people who write down their main goals and carry their list around with them. They don't necessarily refer to it very often, but the act of carrying your goals on a piece of paper is very powerful. Give it a try and see what the results are like.

2 **Understand your motivation.** People retire for different reasons, so it is important to understand your own reasons

If you don't make a clear decision to retire 10 years early, it is unlikely to happen.

for early retirement. Do you want to have more time to spend with your family, see different countries or set up your own small business? Whatever your motivation, have a good reason to retire 10 years early as it will make your journey a lot easier. Even total contempt for your job can be a good enough reason! Your motivation for early retirement is the thing that will keep you going in the years leading up to your retirement date.

> **Your motivation for early retirement is the thing that will keep you going.**

3 **Define what early retirement means to you.** Spend some time thinking about what your lifestyle will look like in retirement. If you are married or in a relationship, then make sure that your partner knows what your vision for retirement is and you know what his or her vision looks like as well. Having a shared vision for early retirement will ensure that you are both pulling in the same direction.

4 **Dismiss the myths about retirement.** There is a lot of nonsense spoken about retirement planning and pensions in particular. Design your plans based on the facts rather than rumours from friends, family or colleagues. It is valuable to listen to opinions from a wide range of people, but make sure that they are not simply repeating what they have heard from an unreliable source elsewhere. Avoid what I call 'golf course investment experts' who are happy to tell you tales of their financial success but probably only after you have missed the boat for that opportunity.

5 **Consider how life expectancy impacts your plans.** Living for longer poses some difficult challenges for retirement planning. Your money has to last for longer during retirement

than it did 50 years ago. This is made worse by the intention to retire 10 years earlier. Living longer calls for careful planning so that you will have the financial resources you need during the retirement phase of your life.

> Living for longer poses some difficult challenges. Your money has to last for longer.

6 **Talk to your parents.** Living for longer means that there is a good chance your parents will be alive well into your retirement. This creates the scenario of the '60-year-old kid' described earlier in the book. Have an open and honest conversation with your parents about your plans for retirement and find out what their own plans look like. It is important to find out at an early stage if they will need any financial assistance from you after you have retired. The provision of long-term care (either at home or in a residential or nursing home) is extremely expensive and requires long-range planning if it is to be covered with comfort.

> Living for longer means that there is a good chance your parents will be alive well into your retirement.

7 **Stack the odds of a longer life in your favour.** While living for longer poses certain challenges for retirement planning, it is actually quite good news! There are numerous lifestyle changes you can make to stack the odds of a long life in your favour. Consider how your eating, smoking, drinking and exercise habits in younger life will shape your life expectancy and health in retirement. Consider making

simple changes now that could have a big impact on your life in the future.

Living for longer is actually quite good news!

8 Forget about life expectancy and plan for the best-case scenario. The problem with average life expectancy is that you might not be very average. It is better to plan for the best-case scenario (living for longer) than it is to plan for the worst-case scenario – an early death. Planning for the latter could see your financial resources running out too early and having to fall back on the State for financial assistance in later life.

Better to plan for the best-case scenario (living for longer) than for an early death.

9 Feel just a little big smug. As a nation, the UK is pretty good at starting early with personal retirement planning. You are likely to already have some plans in place for retirement that will give you a head start. Anything you have already contributed into a pension fund or an investment plan means that you do not have to start from scratch. Feel positive that you have already started to make progress towards an early retirement.

10 Get organised. Being organised will take a lot of the stress out of your journey towards an early retirement. Before you try to start to plan your route to retirement, you should have a general tidying session and take steps to become better organised in the way you run your life. We could all benefit from a simpler life with fewer distractions and more focus.

11 Understand the early retirement roadblocks. There are several things that can get in the way of an early retirement. If you know what these look like, you stand a far better chance of avoiding them. When making your plans for an early retirement, make a list of the things that might get in the way and write down what your plans to avoid these roadblocks look like. As well as the early retirement roadblocks described earlier in this book, we all have personal roadblocks that might get in the way of our own early retirement. Identify these and deal with them at an early stage.

> Stop adopting the 'ostrich' approach to personal financial management.

12 Find out where you are right now. Stop adopting the 'ostrich' approach to personal financial management and take your head out of the sand. This means writing down your income, expenditure, assets and liabilities so that you can see what these numbers all look like and have them in one place. Be honest with yourself about the state of your personal finances and stop avoiding having to open bank statements or credit card bills. They are almost never as bad as you think they will be. It is always better to know where you are so that you can deal with any financial problems as soon as possible than live in blissful ignorance of major financial turmoil that is just building up and up. Face up to your finances today.

13 Build your early retirement toolkit. Get together the things that you will need to retire 10 years early. Earlier in this book you will have read about some suggestions for the things you might need to make the journey a bit easier. Don't spend too much money getting these items together as that money could be better spent on your plans to retire 10 years early.

> Find a good independent financial adviser, you
> will see that his or her services are priceless.

14 Engage the services of a good financial adviser. If you can find a good independent financial adviser, you will see that his or her services are priceless. Regardless of whether you want to mostly delegate your financial planning to the adviser or just use his or her services to implement different financial products on your behalf, you will get good value from the adviser's ability to take an impartial view of your finances and choose the most suitable products from the whole of the market. A good financial adviser can be hard to find, so ask friends, family and colleagues for their recommendations.

15 Understand the benefits of budgeting. Having a well-planned budget that you stick to each month can be one of the most powerful tools in your retirement planning toolkit. It will help you to identify where you are wasting your money on unnecessary expenditure and where this could be reallocated to achieve your plan to retire 10 years early. Having a well-managed budget will help you keep on track.

> Identify where you are wasting your money.

16 Look out for the signs of a bad budget. Not all budgets are born equal. If your own budget is demonstrating some of the signs of a poor budget described earlier in this book, then you need to sit down and review it. The worst budgets I have seen in the past make no allowances for emergency expenditure, so, when this occurs, it throws you straight into the red. A good budget makes your goals more realistic, but a bad budget is almost impossible to follow in the long term.

> **The worst budgets make no allowances for emergency expenditure.**

17 **Make some assumptions.** When you are budgeting and constructing plans for an early retirement, you need to make some assumptions. These are more than educated guesses, but you should review them on a regular basis to ensure that they remain accurate. It is better to review an assumption after a year than wait for 20 years and discover that you were completely wrong. Good financial planning is all about making assumptions and then checking that they were correct.

18 **Think ahead about the money you will spend when you retire.** Your expenditure when you retire is likely to be very different from your expenditure today. Some items will vanish while others will reduce, stay the same or even increase. Work through your budget line by line to establish what is likely to happen to each item of expenditure once you retire. Don't just assume that you will spend less because you are no longer working and the mortgage has been paid off – life in retirement is rarely that simple!

> **Don't just assume that you will spend less.**

19 Find the best way to manage your budget. Different budget management techniques work for different people. If you manage your budget most effectively by keeping cash in envelopes, then stick with that. If you need to open multiple savings accounts for different goals, then stick with that. Just use the budgeting technique that works best for you. This should mean that it is simple to understand and easy to follow.

20 Face up to debt. Debt is the biggest drag on your ability to retire 10 years early. Every pound of debt you have will reduce the money you can put towards your plans for an early retirement. You need to face up to the debt you have and stop making it worse. Relying on credit cards that you cannot repay in full each month means that there is a problem with your budget somewhere. Spending like this is not sustainable in the longer term and it will prevent you from achieving an early retirement.

21 Categorise your debt. Understand your debt and categorise it. You need to know which items of debt are bad debt and which are good debt. It's all debt, but it has different characteristics that are explained earlier in this book. If you know your debt in detail, then you stand a much better chance of clearing it.

Know your debt in detail, then you stand a much better chance of clearing it.

22 Work on clearing your bad debt. Always start by clearing your bad debt. This is the debt that is the most expensive and not helping you to create any wealth. Until you get rid of your overdraft, credit cards, store cards and personal loans, you will find it very difficult to put sufficient financial resources towards your plans for an early retirement. Start with your bad debt and then move on to your good debt.

> **Start with your bad debt and then move on to your good debt.**

23 **Consider clearing your good debt.** Once you have sorted out your bad debt, you can move on to looking at your good debt. This means working out a way to reduce your outstanding mortgage balance. Making regular overpayments will significantly speed up the repayment of your mortgage and reduce the total interest you will have to pay over its life. If you have cash, then consider offsetting this against the mortgage to reduce your monthly interest charges.

> **Making regular overpayments will significantly speed up the repayment of your mortgage.**

24 **Know the difference between a financial product and an investment.** Plans for an early retirement often fall down because of cynical views about the performance of pension plans. A pension is only a financial product. What counts is the contents of that product – the investments. By understanding the difference between a product and the investments within that product, you will be in a position to take greater control over your plans for an early retirement.

25 **Watch out for five things when buying any financial product.** Shopping around for the most suitable financial product is about more than just price. You also need to look for open and transparent charges, high standards of service, a wide

> Selecting a product based *only* on price or performance will always lead to disappointment.

range of investment funds, the financial strength of the provider and flexibility of the product to change as your life evolves. Selecting a product based *only* on price or performance neglects these important criteria and will always lead to disappointment.

26 Use pensions as a foundation for your early retirement planning. For all of the bad press they get, pensions still represent an excellent way to build a tax-efficient fund that can form the basis of your early retirement plans. They do have limitations, but, as long as you understand them, you can plan around them and gain valuable tax benefits on the contributions you make. Don't fear the 'p' word.

> Don't fear the 'p' word.

27 Invest outside of a pension to give yourself greater flexibility. Early retirement planning requires a certain degree of flexibility. The best early retirement plans are made up of a range of pension and non-pension assets. You might not get income tax relief on your non-pension investments, but they

> The best plans are made up of a range of pension and non-pension assets.

are easier to access at an earlier age. Think about retirement planning and not just pension planning when it comes to early retirement.

28 Build your emergency fund. Keeping between three and six months' worth of typical expenditure is a cornerstone of sensible financial planning. Your emergency fund will prevent you from going into the red because of an unexpected item of expenditure. You should make your emergency fund accessible but not too accessible. Once you have built an emergency fund, keep it strictly for emergencies and not anything else!

29 Understand the relationship between risk and reward. When you are investing money, you cannot escape the link between risk and reward – it is unbreakable. Getting more reward from your investments requires that you take greater risks with your money. If you are only comfortable with a more cautious approach to investment, you have to accept that you are likely to get lower returns as a result in the longer term.

30 Consider taking more risk with your early retirement planning. When you have less time until your target retirement date, the conventional investment wisdom suggests that you should take less risk with your money. You should disregard conventional wisdom, though, and consider taking more risk because you need the extra helping hand that higher investment returns can provide.

31 Control risk by means of effective asset allocation. The best way to control the amount of risk you are taking with your plans for early retirement is to diversify using the four main asset classes – cash, fixed-interest securities, property and equities. These all behave differently, so getting the right balance in each asset class is essential. This is also where the majority of investment returns come from. Forget about picking the best company share or investment fund – if you

> The best way to control the amount of risk is to diversify using the four main asset classes.

are not in the right asset class in the first place, you don't stand a chance of making money. Start with asset allocation and the investment returns will follow.

32 **Spend less money!** One way to put more money towards your plans for early retirement is to spend less. Take a long hard look at your budget to see where you could cut your level of expenditure. There are many ways to save money and a few of them are described earlier in this book. Saving money is starting to become a national obsession, with consumers always looking for the best deal or the latest bargain. Become a money saver, too, so that you can move closer towards retiring 10 years early.

33 **Use extreme budgeting for a month to kick-start your spending diet.** Spending one month trying to spend as little as possible is a good way to get started with your early retirement plans. This sort of extreme budgeting, like crash dieting, is not sustainable in the long term, but it does help to focus your mind on a 'spend less, save more' attitude to life that carries over into the months afterwards.

34 **Slash the cost of every financial product you buy.** There is always a big difference between the cheapest and most expensive financial products. Choosing the most expensive product can have a huge impact on the eventual value of your retirement plans. Cheap is not always best, but, in many cases, there is no point in spending more on a product unless you are getting significantly better value for money. Always review the *whole* of the market before buying a financial product as a tied financial adviser will rarely offer the product that is most competitive across *all* areas. Competition in the financial services sector is healthy, so use this to your advantage and save plenty of money.

> Competition in the financial services sector is healthy, so use this to your advantage.

35 Understand the difference between tax evasion and tax avoidance. There is an important distinction between these two terms. The first will land you in serious trouble with the taxman, but the second should be encouraged. To stop paying unnecessary tax you need to legally avoid it at every opportunity.

36 Pay less tax. Some of the simplest tax avoidance measures are also the most effective. Make sure that you are using all of your available tax relief and allowances. We typically overpay tax to the average tune of £160 a year, so paying less can add up to a serious cost saving over the course of your life. Follow the 10 steps that I suggested earlier in the book to make sure you pay less tax.

> We typically overpay tax to the average tune of £160 a year.

37 Get tax relief on pension contributions. The income tax relief available on pension contributions is the most generous gift on offer from the taxman. Basic rate income tax relief is added directly to your pension fund, so more of your money is invested from day one. If you are a higher rate tax payer, you can reclaim the difference between the basic and higher tax rates. This can make a big difference to your overall tax liability at the end of each year and you will be saving towards your early retirement.

38 Reduce the tax you pay on your investments. Once you have used up your tax-efficient investment allowances, it is possible to pay still less tax on your investment returns. I have described five ways to pay less tax on investments earlier in this book.

39 Work out how much money you will need to be able to retire. Once you know the type of lifestyle you are aiming for during retirement, and how much it is likely to cost, you will be able to work out how much money you need to save to achieve that objective. To work this out, you will need to make a series of assumptions. For this reason, make sure that you review your targets and assumptions on a regular basis. If they turn out to be incorrect, then it is better to take corrective action sooner rather than later.

40 Monitor your progress by setting benchmarks. This is an effective way to make sure that your plans remain on track. When reviewing investments for our clients, we use relative and absolute performance benchmarks to measure the success (or otherwise) of a particular investment portfolio. If you do this, it will give you a very useful guide as to how well your own plans are going.

41 Carry out a thorough annual financial review. Put a date in your diary each year to sit down and carry out a formal review of your financial and early retirement plans. Use the structure described earlier in this book to produce a consistent and documented review of your plans. The review can also be used to measure your progress on an annual basis.

42 Sort out your financial paperwork. Most of us hold on to financial paperwork that we don't need. When a new statement comes in, check that it is correct and file it away, but dispose of the statement from last year. Keeping carrier bags full of financial paperwork is not a sign of an organised person who is likely to succeed with any plans for an early retirement. Keep it tidy, keep it organised and you are more likely to stay on track with your plans.

> **Keep it tidy, keep it organised and you are more likely to stay on track with your plans.**

43 Consider the alternatives to early retirement. Not everyone wants to give up work completely and retire early. There are alternatives to consider and the new pension rules offer a lot more flexibility to mix and match income from earnings and your pension than was possible previously. Even if you do not plan to retire 10 years early, you should still follow parts of this plan as doing so will put you in a stronger financial position if the worst, including serious ill health or redundancy, were to happen to you.

44 Make extra years in employment really count. In our later years, we typically earn more and spend less than when we were younger. This means that you should be able to put larger amounts towards your plans for retirement as you get older. Don't rely on this to provide for the majority of your financial plans, though, as the money you invest later in life will not be invested for very long. You should, however, make the most of what you can afford to save towards your retirement when those financial resources become available.

45 Maximise your State pension benefits. While State pension benefits on their own will not allow you to live a wealthy lifestyle during retirement, they are an important foundation for your income in retirement. Find out how much you are likely to receive from the State and consider topping this up with voluntary contributions. Proposed rule changes to the UK State pension system are likely to benefit people who are retiring after 2010.

46 Keep working and still retire. It is possible, and sometimes desirable, to continue to work *and* take pension benefits at the same time. That additional income can either fund a more lavish lifestyle or you can reinvest it for the future. You can recycle excess income as pension contributions, which can be a very tax-efficient use of the money.

47 Earn some extra money. As well as cutting how much you spend each month, consider generating additional income to supplement your plans for an early retirement. Working harder now while you are young and full of energy will enable you to retire earlier than you could otherwise. Improving your performance at work and receiving a pay rise above the rate of inflation can have more of an impact than cutting your expenditure or even extreme budgeting. Managing to combine spending less with earning more puts you on to a real early retirement winner.

> Receiving a pay rise above the rate of inflation can have more of an impact than cutting your expenditure.

48 Keep learning. This book should be simply the starting point for learning how to retire 10 years early. Read widely. The personal finance sections in the weekend papers are full of useful information about how to improve your finances. Also learn by speaking to people you know who have been successful with their plans for retirement.

49 Talk to other people about your plans for an early retirement. Finding other people who are also planning to retire 10 years early will help motivate you to succeed with your own goals. It can be very useful to learn from their experiences and avoid the mistakes that others have made. The Internet is full of forums where people with different financial goals are prepared to discuss their progress. Find a forum, become an active member and learn from the best.

50 **Retire ten years early!** After all this you should be in a far stronger financial position to make retiring 10 years early a reality rather than a dream. Choosing to retire 10 years early starts and ends with the decisions you make about the money you spend and save.

Please do one thing

Thank you for reading this far. The only thing I want every reader of this book to do is make a conscious decision. I want you to decide when you will retire and how you will make this happen. I want you to form a plan and stick to it. All of this starts with a conscious decision.

If, after reading this book and considering the contents, you decide not to take any action, I won't get upset. Doing nothing is also a conscious decision, but at least you will have thought through all of the relevant issues.

Good luck with your plans for an early retirement. This book gives you the knowledge you need to get started. The ability to retire 10 years early now rests with you.

Index